Distillation - Modelling, Simulation and Optimization

Edited by Vilmar Steffen

Published in London, United Kingdom

IntechOpen

Supporting open minds since 2005

Distillation - Modelling, Simulation and Optimization
http://dx.doi.org/10.5772/intechopen.78212
Edited by Vilmar Steffen

Contributors
Vandana Sakhre, Bao The Nguyen, Victor Mazur, Sergey Artemenko, Adriana Téllez-Anguiano, Mario Heras-Cervantes, Gerardo Marx Chávez-Campos, Héctor J. Vergara-Hernández, Juan Anzurez-Marin, Elisa Espinosa-Juárez, Juan Ortega Saavedra, Adriel Sosa, Luis Fernandez, Elena Gómez, Eugénia A. Macedo, Vilmar Steffen

First published in London, United Kingdom, 2019 by IntechOpen
IntechOpen is the global imprint of INTECHOPEN LIMITED, registered in England and Wales, registration number: 11086078, 7th floor, 10 Lower Thames Street, London, EC3R 6AF, United Kingdom
Printed in Croatia

British Library Cataloguing-in-Publication Data
A catalogue record for this book is available from the British Library

Additional hard and PDF copies can be obtained from orders@intechopen.com

Distillation - Modelling, Simulation and Optimization
Edited by Vilmar Steffen
p. cm.
Print ISBN 978-1-78923-915-7
Online ISBN 978-1-78923-916-4
eBook (PDF) ISBN 978-1-83880-287-5

For EU product safety concerns:
IN TECH d.o.o., Prolaz Marije Krucifikse Kozulić 3, 51000 Rijeka, Croatia, info@intechopen.com or visit our website at intechopen.com.

Meet the editor

Professor Vilmar Steffen graduated from high school at Colégio Estadual São José, having received a BSc in Chemical Engineering from the Western Paraná State University – Unioeste (2007), an MSc in Chemical Engineering (dissertation title: Modelling and Simulation of Reactive Distillation Columns) from the Western Paraná State University – Unioeste (2010), and a PhD in Chemical Engineering (thesis title: Determination of Ions Sorption Isotherms Using Poisson-Boltzmann Equation) from the State University of Maringá (2014). He has successfully completed six months of a postdoctoral research fellowship in the Western Paraná State University – Unioeste (2015). Since February 2015, he has been Assistant Professor at the Academic Department of Chemical Engineering (DAENQ) of the Federal Technological University of Paraná (UTFPR) Câmpus Francisco Beltrão – Paraná – Brazil. His research work focuses on process modeling and simulation.

Contents

Preface

Distillation is one of the most used processes for industrial separation, and is responsible for a great part of energy consumption. The correct design and operation of a distillation column can lead to large savings of energy. Having sufficient knowledge to make an efficient column project and establish the best operational conditions needs experience and many tests. These types of tests can be very expensive, and is one of the reasons why it is justified to use process simulation tools, because with simulation tools various virtual tests and process changes can be evaluated at a reduced cost.

A mathematical model is necessary for making a simulation and consequently many simulations are necessary for the optimization of a process. However, the mathematical model must correctly represent the quantities and reflect the state of the studied system, so that simulation and optimization can succeed. During mathematical model construction an engineer must attempt to make the model simpler. This can be done without significant loss of capacity of system properties behavior.

The book is divided into four main sections. The first section contains the introductory chapter. The second section has two chapters dealing with the modeling of the distillation process using solar distillation and batch distillation. The third section has two chapters that discuss topics related to phase equilibrium modeling and simulation, very important steps of distillation process modeling. The last section deals with the modeling, simulation, and optimization of reactive distillation processes, a technique combining both reaction and separation in a single unit operation.

The importance of distillation can be reflected by the number of variations of the process, e.g., batch distillation, solar distillation, vacuum distillation, steam distillation, and fractional distillation. In some cases the mixture being distillated creates a problem in the separation process leading to modifications such as extractive distillation, azeotropic distillation, etc. Attempts to improve product quality can be done by the addition of, e.g., pump-around, side-stripper, etc. Energy saving can be attained by strategies such as vapor compression and vapor recompression. One of the most successful variants of distillation is reactive distillation (also known as reactive distillation with side reactors), a process intensification that has been applied successfully to lots of applications and has been revealed as a promising strategy for recent challenges. This book presents just a small part of the large scientific field involving modeling, simulation, and optimization of distillation.

Vilmar Steffen
Departamento Acadêmico de Engenharia Química,
Universidade Tecnológica Federal do Paraná,
Francisco Beltrão,
Paraná, Brazil

Section 1

Introduction

Chapter 1

Introductory Chapter: Distillation

Vilmar Steffen

1. Modelling, simulation, and optimization of distillation processes

Obtaining a phenomenological model of a process consists on applying law conservations, like mass, energy, and momentum balances and constitutive relations, like vapor-liquid equilibrium, chemical reaction rate, chemical equilibrium relation, etc. A mathematical model, developed to represent (approximately) the real behavior of a process, is very important to analyze an existing plant or to evaluate the technical viability of a new chemical process plant. These analyses and evaluations normally are carried out by making changes in some process parameter and measuring the results of the respective change, in other words, carry out lots of "what if" relations. The analysis of a plant, by simulation, within the development of new processes may frequently show beforehand whether it is technically and economically viable [1].

The solution process of a mathematical model is known as simulation (nowadays, simulation is synonymous of computational simulation). Analyzing a process based only in the mathematical model, is a task almost impossible, but the numerical results of simulation can be easier analyzed. The mathematical model is very important, beyond for simulation and analyses, for the optimization of a process. The mathematical model must correctly represent the quantities and reflect the state of the studied system, only so the simulation and optimization will succeed. In the step of the mathematical model construction, the engineer must analyze if some simplifications, which can make the model simpler (or much simpler), can be adopted without a significant loss in the prediction capacity of system property behavior. However complex a model may be, it cannot represent exactly the real behavior, so some simplifications can be accepted, resulting in a much more simpler model, with little loss in the result quality [2].

The complexity of a distillation column is not due to the material and energy balances that normally are simple equations. This complexity comes from the constitutive relations of chemical reaction (for the case of reactive distillation), mass transfer relation (in a more simplified way, phase equilibrium), and relations to compute the enthalpy. The chemical reaction must be analyzed for chemical equilibrium limitation and chemical reaction rates to evaluate if, in the column dimensions and operation conditions, the desired conversion will be reached. The enthalpies must be precisely evaluated, because it has influence on the heat duties of the condenser and reboiler. And, the thermodynamic property that has the greatest influence on the simulation of separation processes are those related to phase equilibria, for this part is necessary the non-idealities prediction of vapor phase (usually performed with equations of state) and liquid phase (associated with the excess Gibbs energy models). A good phase equilibrium modelling can predict limitations on the separation like those ones caused by azeotrope formation.

The distillation process is the most commonly used in industry to separate chemical mixtures; its applications range from cosmetic and pharmaceutical to petrochemical industries [3] and are responsible for a great part of energy consumption. Evaporation systems are some of the most energy-intensive parts of chemical plants [4], and the needed energy in a distillation column is used in the heat change process occurring in the reboiler. Finding solutions for energy saving has become one of the most demanding issues faced by almost all the governments, decision-makers, and stakeholders all over the world [5]. Energy saving is practiced for improving the efficiency, to minimize fossil and renewable fuels consumption, and to reduce resulting pollution and environmental burdens [4, 6]. This last item is closely related to climate change and other negative environmental impacts. But, high-energy consumption remains a challenge [7]. Fortunately, there are different ways of saving energy. In production, starting with the selection of production process thereby reducing the environmental stress [8]. The energy-efficient policies with renewable energy integration are not an actual trend; this is a requirement for sustainability [9].

A good way to reduce the environmental impacts is using solar energy. Solar distillation (solar stills that user solar radiation in the distillation process) is a method of water purification that can be implemented at low cost and less energy consumption (if compared with conventional processes) and is environmentally friendly.

Process intensification is an effective strategy to achieve increased energy efficiency. Process intensification aims at reducing the mass and heat transfer resistances while overcoming thermodynamic limitations through the integrated design and operation [10]. Recent developments in energy-related research increasingly rely upon simultaneous resource saving and pollution reduction by applying process integration [4]. Process intensification is a feasible way to reduce heat requirement [7]. One of the most common examples of the process intensification field is the reactive distillation, where the integration of reaction and separation is performed. In the cases where reactive distillation has been used, the operating and investment costs are significantly reduced, when compared to the classic set-up of a reactor followed by distillation. Reactive distillation processes offer several important advantages that include the increment of the reaction yield and selectivity, the overcoming of thermodynamic restrictions, and the considerable reduction in energy, water, and solvent consumptions [10]. So, this integration has been successfully applied in several plants. Unfortunately, the modelling and simulation (an important in the process analysis) become a quite complex.

Concluding, it is very important to well design, operate, and control (for keeping the optimal condition operation) a distillation column, which can lead to a large save on energy and raw material consumption. But, having enough knowledge for making an efficient column project and establishing the best operational conditions need much experience and lots of tests on the process in study, and this type of tests can be very expensive; this is one of the reasons that justify the usage of process simulation tools. Analysis based on numerical simulation results (various virtual tests Considering lots of changes in the process parameters) probably will lead to cost reduction or increase in profit.

Author details

Vilmar Steffen
Universidade Tecnológica Federal do Paraná—UTFPR, Francisco Beltrão, Paraná, Brasil

*Address all correspondence to: vilmars@utfpr.edu.br

References

[1] Steffen V, da Silva EA. Steady-state modeling of equilibrium distillation. In: Distillation—Innovative Applications and Modeling. IntechOpen; 2017. Available from: http://www.intechopen.com/books/distillation-innovative-applications-and-modeling/steady-state-modeling-of-equilibrium-distillation

[2] Narváez-García A, Zavala-Loría JC, Ruiz-Marín A, Canedo-López Y. Short-cut methods for multicomponent batch distillation. In: Distillation—Innovative Applications and Modeling. IntechOpen; 2017. Available from: http://www.intechopen.com/books/distillation-innovative-applications-and-modeling/short-cut-methods-for-multicomponent-batch-distillation

[3] Téllez-Anguiano A d C, Heras-Cervantes M, Anzurez-Marín J, Chávez-Campos GM, JAG G. Mathematical modelling of batch distillation columns: A comparative analysis of non-linear and fuzzy models. In: Distillation—Innovative Applications and Modeling. IntechOpen; 2017. Available from: http://www.intechopen.com/books/distillation-innovative-applications-and-modeling/mathematical-modelling-of-batch-distillation-columns-a-comparative-analysis-of-non-linear-and-fuzzy

[4] Klemeš JJ, Varbanov PS. Heat transfer improvement, energy saving, management and pollution reduction. Energy. 2018;**162**:267-271. [Accessed: 14 June 2019]. Available from: https://www.sciencedirect.com/science/article/pii/S0360544218315226#bib29

[5] MAA M. Saving energy through using green rating system for building commissioning. Energy Procedia. 2019;**162**:369-378. [Accessed: 14 June 2019]. Available from: https://www.sciencedirect.com/science/article/pii/S1876610219313979

[6] Čuček L, Klemeš JJ, Kravanja Z. Overview of environmental footprints. In: Assessing and Measuring Environmental Impact and Sustainability. Elsevier; 2015. pp. 131-193. Available from: https://linkinghub.elsevier.com/retrieve/pii/B9780127999685000051

[7] Jin H, Liu P, Li Z. Energy-efficient process intensification for post-combustion CO_2 capture: A modeling approach. Energy. 2018;**158**:471-483. [Accessed: 2019 June 14]. Available from: https://www.sciencedirect.com/science/article/pii/S0360544218311101?via%3Dihub

[8] Tekkaya AE. Energy saving by manufacturing technology. Procedia Manufacturing. 2018;**21**:392-396. [Accessed: 14 June 2019]. Available from: https://www.sciencedirect.com/science/article/pii/S2351978918301756

[9] Romero RJ, Silva-Sotelo S. Energy evaluation of the use of an absorption heat pump in water distillation process. In: Distillation—Innovative Applications and Modeling. IntechOpen; 2017. Available from: http://www.intechopen.com/books/distillation-innovative-applications-and-modeling/energy-evaluation-of-the-use-of-an-absorption-heat-pump-in-water-distillation-process

[10] Segovia-Hernández JG, Hernández S, Bonilla Petriciolet A. Reactive distillation: A review of optimal design using deterministic and stochastic techniques. Chemical Engineering and Processing Process Intensification. 2015;**97**:134-143 Available from: http://dx.doi.org/10.1016/j.cep.2015.09.004

Section 2

Distillation

Chapter 2

Fuzzy Logic Modeling and Observers Applied to Estimate Compositions in Batch Distillation Columns

Mario Heras-Cervantes, Gerardo Marx Chávez-Campos, Héctor Javier Vergara Hernández, Adriana del Carmen Téllez-Anguiano, Juan Anzurez-Marin and Elisa Espinosa-Juárez

Abstract

In this chapter, the analysis and design of a fuzzy observer based on a Takagi-Sugeno model of a batch distillation column are presented. The observer estimates the molar compositions and temperatures of the light component in the distillation column considering a binary mixture. This estimation aims to allow monitoring the physical variables in the process to improve the quality of the distillated product as well as to detect failures that could affect the system performance. The Takagi-Sugeno fuzzy model is based on eight linear subsystems determined by three premise variables: the opening percentage of the reflux valve and the liquid molar composition of the light element of the binary mixture in the boiler and in the condenser. The stability analysis and the observer gains are obtained by linear matrix inequalities (LMIs). The observer is validated by MATLAB® simulations using real data obtained from a distillation column to verify the observer's convergence and analyze its response under system disturbances.

Keywords: Takagi-Sugeno modeling, fuzzy observers, composition estimation, distillation column

1. Introduction

Distillation is the process to separate chemical substances most used in the industry, with the petrochemical (petroleum products) [1] and food (alcoholic beverages production) industries being the most important due to the current people lifestyle in which the daily use of petroleum fuels is essential for both transport and energy generation.

Fractional distillation is used to separate homogeneous liquid mixtures in which the difference between the boiling points of the components is less than 25°C. Each of the separate components is called fractions. In general, there are two operating modes: continuous and batch. In the continuous mode, the feeding of the liquid mixture and the extraction of the distilled product are carried out continuously. In the batch distillation, the mixture is initially deposited in the boiler; at the end of the process, the distillate and bottom product are extracted.

The batch operation is mainly used to separate small amounts of mixture, to obtain different qualities of the distilled product from the same mixture, or to separate multicomponent mixtures.

A batch distillation column is not operated using constant parameters; the control actions are continuously adjusted according to the state of the distillation; therefore, monitoring and controlling all the variables of the process are essential to improve the quality and quantity of the distilled product, as well as to guarantee the safety of the process and the operators. To fulfill or facilitate this objective, it is necessary to implement control techniques such as models, observers, and controllers.

In the literature, modeling and control techniques such as estimators, observers, fault detection systems, and control systems are applied to distillation columns in order to obtain a better analysis and understanding of the dynamics of the process, improving the quality of the distilled product and enhancing the user safety, among other tasks.

Distillation column simplified models present the basic principles of the process and its operation taking into account several considerations to describe the dynamics of the system in a simpler but understandable form. Authors in [2] present a simplified model of a binary distillation column, based on the liquid-vapor equilibrium of the binary mixture and the mass balance considering all the elements of the distillation column as plates.

Authors in [3] design a model based on the existence of the liquid and vapor molar fluids that vary in each column plate; the compositions of the bottom product and the distilled product are estimated using a dynamic model based on the mass and component balances. In [4] a low-order model of an ideal multicomponent distillation using the theory of nonlinear wave propagation is presented. Authors in [5] present a low-order model for a reactive multicomponent distillation column, in addition to designing a predictive control to obtain the best quality of the distilled product.

Rigorous models are more complete because they represent plate by plate the element balance of phases in each element of the distillation column (boiler, condenser, and plates). In these models, the mathematic expressions are determined by a series of differential equations given by mass, light component, or energy balances depending on the application, the control strategy, or the operation type. An important advantage of the rigorous modeling is the high resolution of the dynamics, having the disadvantage of combining a greater number of variables and expressions that make difficult the design, simulation, and implementation of controllers.

In [6], a model based on neural networks is presented in order to optimize the energy efficiency in a binary distillation column. Authors in [7] present a model of a binary distillation column based on neural networks. The neural network training and validation are performed using real data from a nine-plate pilot plant for a mixture of methanol and water. Authors in [8] present the simulation and optimization of a rigorous model for a batch reactive distillation column. Authors in [9] present the design and simulation of a discrete Kalman filter to estimate the molar compositions of the light component in a batch distillation column.

Generally, the light component composition measurement is performed offline using expensive instruments, so the implementation of state observers to estimate online this composition has become a frequent and important task. Authors in [10–12] present high-gain observers to estimate the light component composition in all the distillation column plates from the measurement of the temperature of some plates and the column actual inputs.

Due to the different distillation types and their mathematical representation, there are different types of observers for different applications. In [13] the authors present a discrete-time D-LPV observer to estimate sensors and actuators states and faults, using the H∞ approach applied to the estimation error.

In [14], the authors present a pair of extended Luenberger observers (complete and reduced order) to estimate the compositions of a multicomponent mixture from temperature measurements of the distillation column plates. The observers' gains are calculated from the location of the closed-loop eigenvalues using a mathematical software.

In [15], a full-order nonlinear observer is presented to estimate the composition and temperatures of a distillation column. A nonlinear model obtained by the mass balance in each plate of the column is used, resulting in a set of high-order differential equations with nonlinear terms. The observer is validated in simulation to demonstrate his behavior and his robustness. The parametric representation or identification is another methodology used to estimate certain variables of the distillation columns, as presented in [16, 17].

The difficulty of designing and implementing the observers lies mainly in the nonlinear dynamics of the distillation column; thus, having a linear system would facilitate the design of observers and controllers to implement control strategies such as fault detection and diagnosis systems and automatic control and tolerant control in order to improve the performance and safety of the process, as well as the quality of the distilled product.

The Takagi-Sugeno fuzzy modeling is a tool to model and control complex systems using a nonlinear system decomposition in a multi-model structure formed by linear and not necessarily independent and fuzzy logic models [18, 19], where the representation of the nonlinear system is achieved by a weighted summation of the whole subsystems. The Takagi-Sugeno representation provides a solution to solve the problems in the design and implementation of control strategies for nonlinear systems.

In [20], the authors propose a methodology to design control techniques for systems represented in the Takagi-Sugeno form. In [21] the identification of a model of a binary distillation column, based on fuzzy models, taking into account 6 system inputs and 2 outputs for 64 rules is presented. The model is simulated using real data to validate its performance.

Authors in [22] present a controller of the molar composition of the distilled and bottom products for a binary distillation column using neural networks and fuzzy logic (ANFIS) based on a 2×2 MIMO system. In [23] an adaptive PID controller based on Takagi-Sugeno modeling to control the distilled and bottom products of a binary distillation column is presented.

Due to the close relationship between the fuzzy representation of nonlinear systems and the theory of linear matrix inequalities, different works based on both techniques have been developed, allowing to find solutions to the calculations corresponding to the observer and controller gains and the Lyapunov stability analysis. In [24], a methodology to design observers and controllers for a fuzzy system is proposed.

The main contribution of this work is the design of a fuzzy observer based on a Takagi-Sugeno model to estimate the molar compositions and temperatures of the light component in each plate of a binary distillation column. The observer performance is validated for applications such as system monitoring and fault detection.

2. Takagi-Sugeno fuzzy model for a batch distillation column

The objective of a batch distillation process is to separate two or more elements from a mixture, where the most volatile element is obtained as the distilled product. The equipment used to carry out the distillation process is the distillation columns or the distillation pilot plants, as shown in **Figure 1**.

A distillation column is composed by a boiler that provides the heat necessary to evaporate the mixture to be distilled; the body of the column is formed by $n-2$ plates, where a partial separation of the mixture is performed due to the phase equilibrium and a condenser that provides the necessary cooling to convert the distilled product to liquid [11].

Due to the high cost of the distillation columns and the amount of energy required in a distillation process, it is necessary to design adequate control strategies to monitor the main process variables and detect sensor and actuator faults to improve the quality of the distilled product and the safety of the process and the user.

2.1 Binary distillation column nonlinear model

The mathematical model of a distillation column consists of a set of differential equations that represent the dynamics of each plate of the column. Usually, the model of a distillation column is based on the balance of the light component in all the plates [10]. The model of a distillation column that considers a binary mixture as well as constant vapor and liquid flows through all columns is shown in Eq. (1):

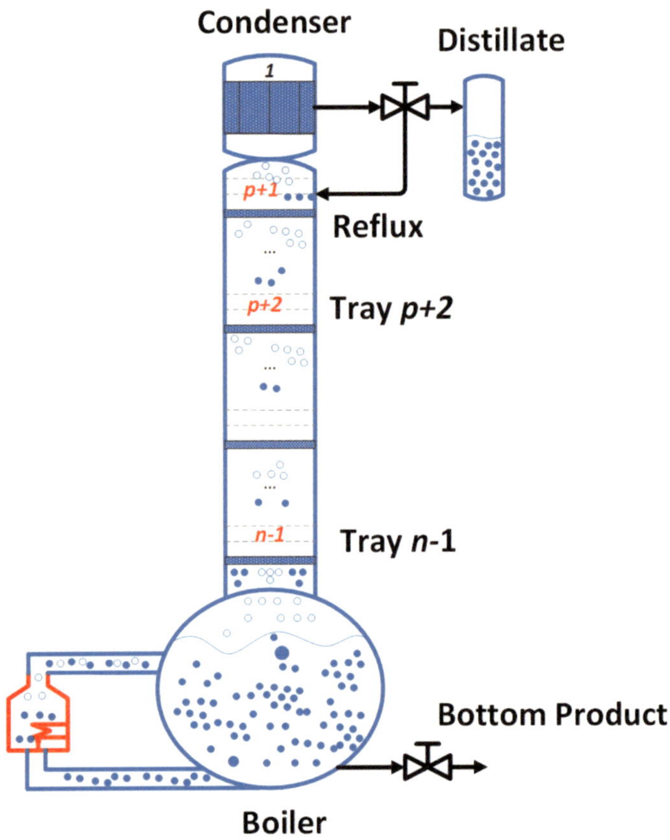

Figure 1.
Distillation column.

$$\frac{dx_i}{dt} = \frac{V(y_{i+1} - y_i) + L(x_{i-1} - x_i)}{M_i} \tag{1}$$

where V is the vapor molar flow, L is the liquid molar flow, M is the retained mass, x_i is the liquid composition in plate i, and y_i is the vapor composition in plate i.

The dynamic representation of a distillation column is based on submodels of the light component balance in each element of the column.

For the condenser, numbered as plate 1, Eq. (2) shows:

$$\frac{dx_1}{dt} = \frac{Vy_{i+1} - Lx_{i-1} - Dx}{M_1} \tag{2}$$

For the intermediate plates of the body of the distillation column, Eq. (3) shows:

$$\frac{dx_i}{dt} = \frac{V(y_{i+1} - y_i) + L(x_{i-1} - x_i)}{M_i} \tag{3}$$

where $i = 2, 3 \ldots n - 1$.

For the boiler, numbered as plate 1, Eq. (4) shows:

$$\frac{dx_n}{dt} = \frac{V(x_n - y_n) + L(x_{n-1} - x_n)}{M_n} \tag{4}$$

where D is the distilled product and n is the total number of plates.

2.1.1 Distillation column state-space model

The state-space dynamics of the distillation column, considering as states the light component composition in all the plates and as control inputs to the heating power, Q_f, and the reflux, R_f, is expressed in Eq. (5):

$$\dot{x} = A \begin{pmatrix} x_1 \\ x_2 \\ \vdots \\ x_{n-1} \\ x_n \end{pmatrix} + B \begin{pmatrix} Rf \\ Qb \end{pmatrix} \tag{5}$$

where A and B matrixes are defined by

$$A = \begin{pmatrix} & & -\frac{(V+D)}{M_i} & \frac{V \cdot G(x_i \alpha_i)}{M_i} & \cdots & 0 \quad 0 \\ & & \frac{L}{M_i} & -\frac{V \cdot G(x_{i+1}\alpha_{i+1}) - L}{M_i} & \cdots & 0 \quad 0 \\ & & & \vdots & & \vdots \\ \vdots & \vdots & \cdots & & & \\ & & & -\frac{V \cdot G(x_{n-1}\,\alpha_{n-1}) - L}{M_{n-1}} & & \frac{V \cdot G(x_n\,\alpha_n)}{M_{n-1}} \\ 0 & 0 & \cdots & & & \\ 0 & 0 & \cdots & \frac{L}{M_n} & & -\frac{L}{M_n} \end{pmatrix}$$

$$B = \begin{pmatrix} \frac{Lx_1}{M_1} & 0 \\ & 0 \\ 0 & \vdots \\ \vdots & 0 \\ 0 & \frac{x_n(1 - G(x_n\, \alpha_n))}{\left(H_i^{vap} x_n + H_j^{vap}(1 - x_n)M_n\right)} \\ 0 & \end{pmatrix}$$

where the molar fluids of liquid, L, and vapor, V, are determined by Eqs. (6) and (7):

$$V = \frac{Q_b}{H_i^{vap} x_n + H_j^{vap}(1 - x_n)} \quad (6)$$

$$L = \left(1 - R_f\right)V \quad (7)$$

where H_i^{vap} is the light component vapor enthalpy, H_j^{vap} is the heavy component vapor enthalpy, and x_n is the light component composition in the boiler.

The $G(x_i, \alpha_i)$function is determined by the light component composition (x_i), the relative volatility (α_i), the saturation pressure $\left(P_i^{sat}\right)$, the pressure in the column P_T, the vapor molar (V), and the activity coefficient (γ_i), as expressed in Eq. (8):

$$G(x_i, \alpha_i) = \frac{VP_i^{sat}\gamma_i}{P_T} \quad (8)$$

2.2 Distillation column Takagi-Sugeno model

The Takagi-Sugeno model is the fuzzy representation of a nonlinear model obtained from the linear subsystems interpolation according to fuzzy rules having the form (Eq. 9):

Model *i* rule

If $z_i\ (t)$ is M_{i1} and ... and $z_p(t)$ is M_{p1}

Then (9)

$$\dot{x}(t) = A_i x(t) + B_i u(t)$$

$$i = 1, 2, \ldots, r$$

where $z_i(t) \sim z_p(t)$ is the premise variables, $M_{i1} \sim M_{p1}$ is the fuzzy sets, r is the number of linear subsystems, $x(t)$ is the state vector, $u(t)$ is the input vector, $A_i$is the linear submodel state matrices, and B_i is the input vector for each subsystem.

Each consecutive linear equation represented by $A_i x(t) + B_i u(t)$ is called a subsystem and represents an operating point of the nonlinear system.

Given the pair $(x(t); u(t))$, the complete fuzzy model is obtained by using a singleton fuzifier, product-type inference mechanism, and center of gravity as a defuser, as described in Eq. (10):

$$\begin{aligned} x(t) &= \frac{\sum_{i=1}^{r} w_i(z(t))(A_i\, x(t) + B_i\, u(t))}{\sum_{i=1}^{r} w_i(z(t))} \\ &= \sum_{i=1}^{r} h_i(z(t))(A_i\, x(t) + B_i\, u(t)) \\ y(t) &= \frac{\sum_{i=1}^{r} w_i(z(t))(C_i\, x(t))}{\sum_{i=1}^{r} w_i(z(t))} = \sum_{i=1}^{r} h_i(z(t))(C_i\, x(t)) \end{aligned} \quad (10)$$

where the vector for p premise variables $z(t)$ is defined by Eq. (11):

$$z(t) = [z_1(t), z_2(t), \cdots, z_p(t)] \tag{11}$$

In addition, the calculated weight $w_i(z(t))$ for each i rule from the membership functions is defined by Eq. (12):

$$w_i(z(t)) = \prod_{j=1}^{p} M_{ij} z_j(t) \tag{12}$$

and the normalized weight h_i for each rule is defined by Eq. (13):

$$h_i(z(t)) = \frac{w_i(z(t))}{\sum_{i=1}^{r} w_i(z(t))} \tag{13}$$

2.3 Fuzzy observer

According to the structure of the fuzzy observer [24–26] expressed in Eq. (14),

$$\begin{gathered} \dot{\hat{x}}(t) = \sum_{i=1}^{r} h_i(z(t))(A_i x(t) + B_i u(t) + K_i(e(t))) \\ \hat{y} = \sum_{i=1}^{r} h_i(z(t))(C_i \hat{x}(t)) \end{gathered} \tag{14}$$

The estimation error is determined by Eq. (15):

$$e(t) = y(t) - \hat{y}(t) \tag{15}$$

The fuzzy observer stability is demonstrated if each A_i, C_i pair is observable and P complies with the Lyapunov equation expressed in Eq. (16):

$$P_i \overline{A}_i + \overline{A}_i{}' P_i < 0 \tag{16}$$

where

$$\overline{A}_i = A_i - K_i C_i$$

In [25], the demonstration that the observer is stable is presented as long as a positive definite matrix P that satisfies the system of linear matrix inequalities (LMIs) is found, as shown in Eq. (17):

$$\begin{gathered} P > 0 \\ N_i > 0 \\ A_i' P - C_i' N_i' + P A_i - N_i C_i < 0 \\ A_i' P - C_j' N_i' + P A_i - N_i C_j + P A_j' - C_i' N_j' + P A_j - N_j C_i < 0 \\ i < j \end{gathered} \tag{17}$$

The observer gains are defined by the LMI systems solution defined in Eq. (18):

$$K_i = P_i^{-1} N_i \tag{18}$$

3. Case of study: EDF-1000 distillation pilot plant

As a case of study, an EDF-1000 distillation pilot plant is used (**Figure 2**), consisting of 11 perforated plates, having 7 RTD (PT100) temperature sensors

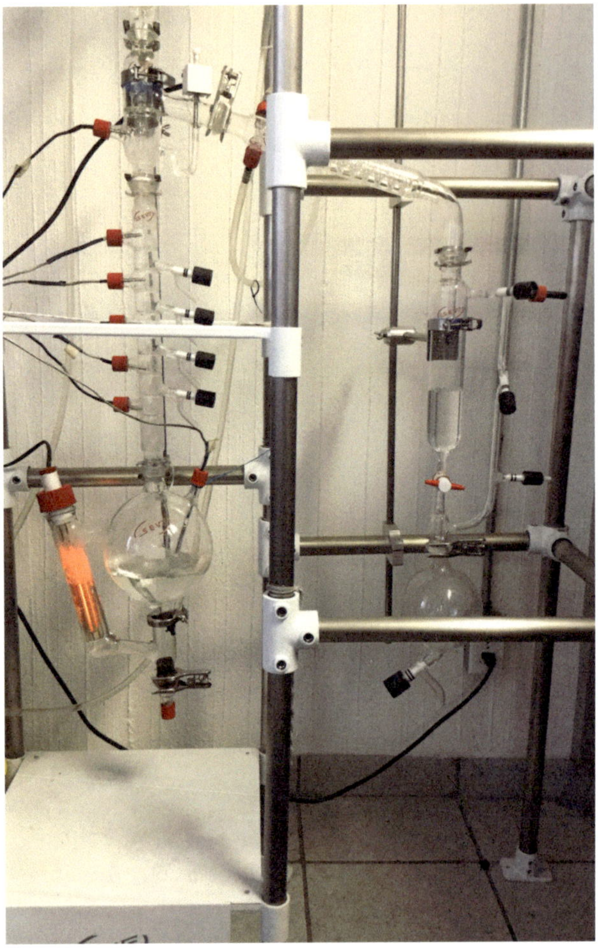

Figure 2.
EDF-1000 distillation pilot plant.

located in the condenser (plate 1); in plates 2, 4, 6, 8, and 10; and in the boiler (plate 11).

The boiler is composed of a 2-L tank to contain the mixture and a side tank to contain a 300-watt heating resistance.

3.1 Case of study: state-space nonlinear model

The following assumptions are considered in the EDF-1000 distillation pilot plant to simplify the designing state without significantly affecting the dynamics and precision of the model:

- Constant pressure in the column.
- Liquid output flows in the column.
- No vapor retention.
- Vapor and liquid balance in all the column plates.
- Adiabatic distillation column.
- Batch operation type.

Eq. (19) shows the mathematical model of a batch-type 11-plate EDF-1000 distillation pilot plant for an ethanol-water mixture, considering the compositions in each plate $(x_1, x_2, \cdots x_{10}, x_{11})$, where the condenser composition is x_1 and the boiler composition is x_{11}; in addition, the control inputs are the heating power Q_f and the reflux R_f:

$$\dot{x} = A\begin{pmatrix} x_1 \\ x_2 \\ \vdots \\ x_{10} \\ x_{11} \end{pmatrix} + B\begin{pmatrix} Rf \\ Qb \end{pmatrix} \qquad y = C\begin{pmatrix} x_1 \\ x_2 \\ \vdots \\ x_{10} \\ x_{11} \end{pmatrix} \tag{19}$$

where A and B matrixes are defined by

$$A = \begin{pmatrix} -\frac{(V+D)}{M_1} & \frac{V\cdot G(x_2\alpha_2)}{M_1} & \cdots & 0 & 0 \\ \frac{L}{M_2} & -\frac{V\cdot G(x_3\alpha_3)-L}{M_2} & \cdots & 0 & 0 \\ \vdots \quad \vdots & \cdots & \vdots & & \vdots \\ 0 \quad 0 & \cdots & -\frac{V\cdot G(x_{10}\alpha_{10})-L}{M_{10}} & & \frac{V\cdot G(x_{11}\alpha_{11})}{M_{10}} \\ 0 \quad 0 & \cdots & \frac{L}{M_{11}} & & -\frac{L}{M_{11}} \end{pmatrix}$$

$$B = \begin{pmatrix} \frac{Lx_1}{M_1} & 0 \\ 0 & 0 \\ \vdots & \vdots \\ 0 & 0 \\ 0 & \frac{x_{11}(1-G(x_{11}\alpha_{11}))}{(H^{vap}_{Eth}x_{11} + H^{vap}_{H20}(1-x_{11})M_{11})} \end{pmatrix}$$

where the output matrix is defined by an 11×11 identity matrix as shown in Eq. (20).

$$C = \begin{pmatrix} 1 & 0 & \cdots & 0 & 0 \\ 0 & 1 & \cdots & \vdots & 0 \\ \vdots & \vdots & \ddots & \vdots & \vdots \\ 0 & 0 & \cdots & 0 & 1 \end{pmatrix} \tag{20}$$

3.2 Case of study: Takagi-Sugeno fuzzy model

The state-space model of the case of study expressed in Eq. (10) contains nonlinearities in the A and B matrices since both are dependent on the states; in addition, the reflux input (Rf) disturbs all the states of the system (compositions) when it is activated.

The premise variables considered in the fuzzy model are the reflux valve opening percentage ($z_3 = Rf$) due to its effect in all the states of the system; the light component composition in the condenser ($z_2 = x_1$), where the distillate product is obtained; and the light component composition in the boiler ($z_1 = x_{11}$), where the original mixture is located; besides, the boiler is directly related to the heating power (one of the system input variables) that provides the energy required to evaporate the mixture.

According to the steady-state dynamics of the distillation column, trapezoidal-type membership functions are chosen with two rules for each one, as expressed mathematically in Eqs. (21) and (22). This type of function is selected because it allows a greater range in the universe of discourse, where the belonging degree of belonging is 1, which prevents an oscillation when the states stabilize:

$$M1 = \begin{cases} 1, z < a \\ \frac{b-z}{b-a}, a \le z \le b \\ 0, z > b \end{cases} \tag{21}$$

$$M2 = \begin{cases} 0, z < a \\ \frac{z-a}{b-a}, a \le z \le b \\ 1, z > b \end{cases} \tag{22}$$

The number of subsystems of the Takagi-Sugeno fuzzy model is dependent on the number of combinations that the membership functions have; for the case of study considering three premise variables ($z_1 = x_{11}, z_2 = x_1$, and $z_3 = Rf$), each one with two rules (z_{imax} and z_{imin}), the number of subsystems is $2^3 = 8$.

Model 1 rule

If $z_1(t)$ is $M1, z_2(t)$ is $M3$ *and* $z_3(t)$ is $M5$

Then

$$\dot{x}(t) = A_1x(t) + B_1u(t)$$
$$y = C_1x(t)$$

Model 2 rule

If $z_1(t)$ is $M1, z_2(t)$ is and $M3$ $z_2(t)$ is $M6$

Then

$$\dot{x}(t) = A_2x(t) + B_2u(t)$$
$$y = C_2x(t)$$

Model 3 rule

If $z_1(t)$ is $M1, z_2(t)$ is $M4$ *and*$z_3(t)$ is $M5$

Then

$$\dot{x}(t) = A_3x(t) + B_3u(t)$$
$$y = C_3x(t)$$

Model 4 rule

If $z_1(t)$ is $M1$, $z_2(t)$ is and $M4$ $z_2(t)$ is $M6$

Then

$$\begin{aligned}\dot{x}(t) &= A_4x(t) + B_4u(t)\\ y &= C_4x(t)\end{aligned}$$

Model 5 rule

If $z_1(t)$ is $M2$, $z_2(t)$ is $M3$ *and* $z_3(t)$ is $M5$

Then

$$\begin{aligned}\dot{x}(t) &= A_5x(t) + B_5u(t)\\ y &= C_5x(t)\end{aligned}$$

Model 6 rule

If $z_1(t)$ is $M2$, $z_2(t)$ is and $M3$ $z_2(t)$ is $M6$

Then

$$\begin{aligned}\dot{x}(t) &= A_6x(t) + B_6u(t)\\ y &= C_6x(t)\end{aligned}$$

Model 7 rule

If $z_1(t)$ is $M2$, $z_2(t)$ is $M4$ *and* $z_3(t)$ is $M5$

Then

$$\begin{aligned}\dot{x}(t) &= A_7x(t) + B_7u(t)\\ y &= C_7x(t)\end{aligned}$$

Model 8 rule

If $z_1(t)$ is $M2$, $z_2(t)$ is and $M4$ $z_2(t)$ is $M6$

Then

$$\begin{aligned}\dot{x}(t) &= A_8x(t) + B_8u(t)\\ y &= C_8x(t)\end{aligned}$$

where $M1$ and $M2$ are fuzzy sets for $z_1(t)$, $M3$ and $M4$ are fuzzy sets for $z_2(t)$, and $M5$ and $M6$ are fuzzy sets for $z_3(t)$.

According to the fuzzy rules, the Takagi-Sugeno fuzzy model of the EDF-100 distillation pilot plant is expressed in Eq. (23):

$$\begin{aligned}\dot{x}(t) &= \sum_{i=1}^{8} h_i(z(t))(A_ix(t) + B_iu(t))\\ y(t) &= \sum_{i=1}^{8} h_i(z(t))(C_ix(t))\end{aligned} \tag{23}$$

3.3 Case of study: fuzzy observer

From the general structure of the fuzzy observer presented in Eq. (14) and the fuzzy Takagi-Sugeno model expressed in Eq. (9), the fuzzy observer for the 11-plate distillation column is expressed in Eq. (24):

$$\dot{\hat{x}}(t) = \sum_{i=1}^{8} h_i(z(t))(A_i x(t) + B_i u(t) + K_i(e(t)))$$
$$\hat{y} = \sum_{i=1}^{8} h_i(z(t))(C_i \hat{x}(t)) \tag{24}$$

The fuzzy observer scheme proposed for the distillation column of the case study is shown in **Figure 3**, taking as inputs the heating power and the reflux action; the estimated states are the molar compositions in all the plates, and the measured outputs are the temperatures in the condenser; in plates 2, 4, 6, 8, and 10; and in the boiler.

Using the LMI system for eight rules, the LMI system for the fuzzy observer is obtained. The LMI's characteristics of each function are expressed in Eq. (25):

$$\begin{aligned} A_1'P - C_1'N_1' + PA_1 - N_1C_1 < 0 \\ A_2'P - C_2'N_2' + PA_2 - N_2C_2 < 0 \\ \vdots \\ A_7'P - C_7'N_7' + PA_7 - N_7C_7 < 0 \\ A_8'P - C_8'N_8' + PA_8 - N_8C_8 < 0 \end{aligned} \tag{25}$$

The LMIs that represent the membership functions overlaps are expressed in Eq. (26):

$$\begin{aligned} A_1'P - C_2'N_1' + PA_1 - N_1C_2 + PA_2' - C_1'N_2' + PA_2 - N_2C_1 < 0 \\ A_1'P - C_3'N_1' + PA_1 - N_1C_3 + PA_3' - C_1'N_3' + PA_3 - N_3C_1 < 0 \\ \vdots \\ A_1'P - C_7'N_1' + PA_1 - N_1C_7 + PA_7' - C_1'N_7' + PA_7 - N_7C_1 < 0 \\ A_2'P - C_3'N_2' + PA_2 - N_2C_3 + PA_3' - C_2'N_3' + PA_3 - N_3C_2 < 0 \\ A_2'P - C_4'N_2' + PA_2 - N_2C_4 + PA_4' - C_2'N_4' + PA_4 - N_4C_2 < 0 \\ \vdots \\ A_2'P - C_7'N_2' + PA_2 - N_2C_7 + PA_7' - C_2'N_7' + PA_7 - N_7C_2 < 0 \\ A_3'P - C_4'N_3' + PA_3 - N_3C_4 + PA_4' - C_3'N_4' + PA_4 - N_4C_3 < 0 \\ A_3'P - C_5'N_3' + PA_3 - N_3C_5 + PA_5' - C_3'N_5' + PA_5 - N_5C_3 < 0 \\ \vdots \\ A_6'P - C_7'N_6' + PA_6 - N_6C_7 + PA_7' - C_6'N_7' + PA_7 - N_7C_6 < 0 \\ A_7'P - C_8'N_7' + PA_7 - N_7C_8 + PA_8' - C_7'N_8' + PA_8 - N_8C_7 < 0 \end{aligned} \tag{26}$$

where P is positive definite diagonal matrix $P > 0$ of 11×11 dimension, and N is an auxiliary matrix dependent on the number of states (11) and the measured outputs (7), resulting in a 7×11 dimension.

The resulting system of 36 LMIs is solved using the MATLAB® *lmiedit* tool. Once the LMI system is solved, with $P > 0$ to guarantee the closed-loop stability of each subsystem, the K_i gains are calculated in Eq. (27):

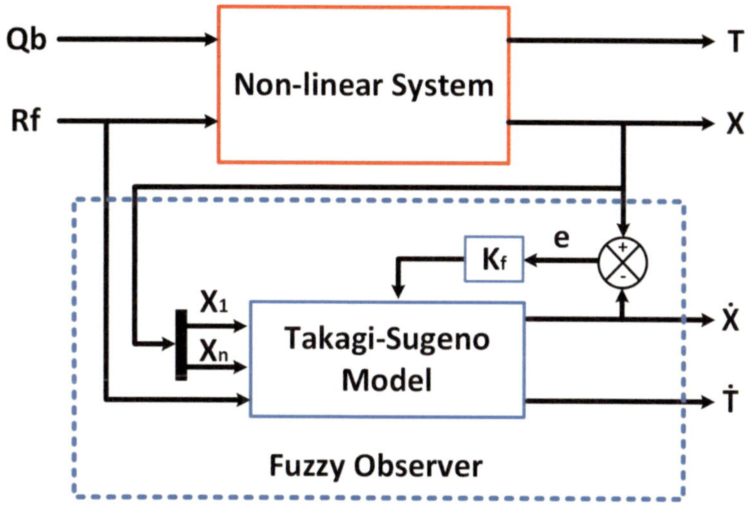

Figure 3.
Observer scheme.

$$\begin{aligned} K_1 &= P^{-1}N_1 \\ K_2 &= P^{-1}N_2 \\ &\vdots \\ K_7 &= P^{-1}N_7 \\ K_8 &= P^{-1}N_8 \end{aligned} \tag{27}$$

4. Results and discussion

The fuzzy observer validation is performed using real data from a distillation process; the main characteristics are shown in **Tables 1** and **2**.

The process operates during 50 min, taking the initial compositions $x(0) = [0.8555, 0.8525, 0.8480, 0.8412, 0.8309, 0.8148, 0.7896, 0.7483, 0.6767, 0.5369, 0.2300]$ in steady state.

Parameter	Magnitude	Units
EtOH volume in the boiler	1000	ml
H_2O volume in the boiler	1000	ml
Process total pressure	662	mmHg

Table 1.
Process parameters.

Parameter	Ethanol	Water	Units
Density (p_i)	0.789	1	kg/m^3
Molecular weight (W_i)	46.069	18.0528	g/mol
Boiling temperature (T_{bi})	78.4	100	°C

Table 2.
Mixture parameters.

The system input signals used in the validation stage are the reflux signal, considering an opening percentage of 20%, starting at the 5 min and lasting 30 min, and the heating power.

Figure 4 shows the light component compositions calculated by the nonlinear model in the 11 plates of the distillation column; this simulation is carried out considering no disturbances in the system.

Figure 5 shows the composition estimated by the observer with initial conditions different from the nonlinear model. The composition initial conditions of the observer are $\hat{x}(0) = [0.8555, 0.8525, 0.8480, 0.8412, 0.8309, 0.8148, 0.7896, 0.7483, 0.6767, 0.5369, 0.2300]$. The convergence time of the observer is 48 sec.

Figure 6 shows the result of the fuzzy observer simulation considering a disturbance in the plate 6 composition.

Figure 7 shows the plate 6 composition estimated by the fuzzy observer and the comparison with the nonlinear model to verify the observer's convergence.

Figure 8 shows the simulation of the compositions estimated by the fuzzy observer under seven perturbations in the composition of plates 4, 6, and 8.

In **Figure 9**, a comparison between the light component compositions in plates 4, 6, and 8 is shown to verify the convergence of the fuzzy observer with the nonlinear model.

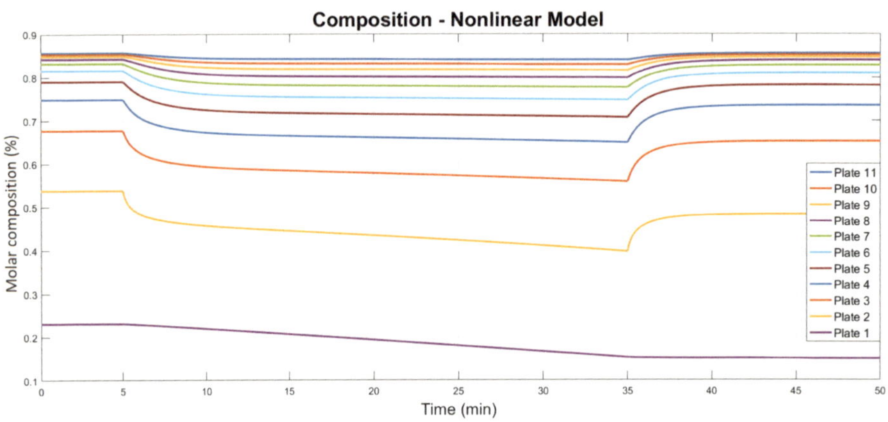

Figure 4.
Light component composition, nonlinear model.

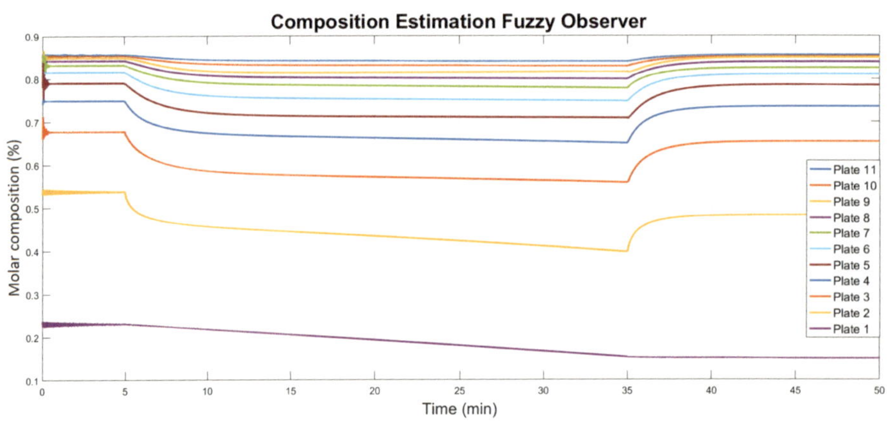

Figure 5.
Light component estimated by the observer. Different initial conditions.

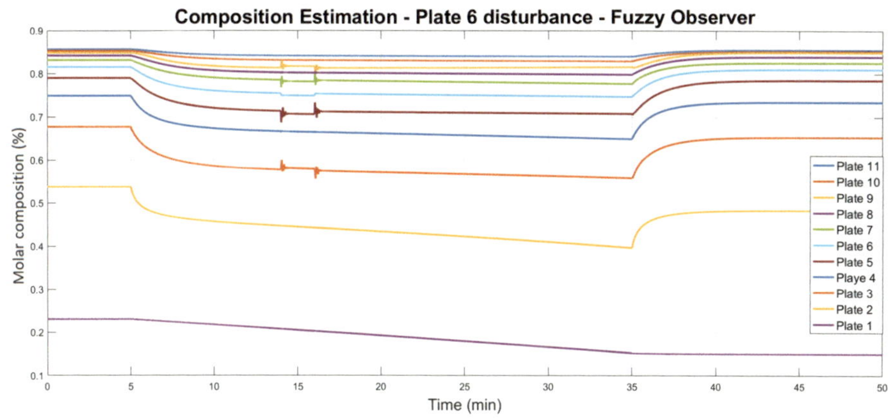

Figure 6.
Plate 6 light component estimation under disturbance.

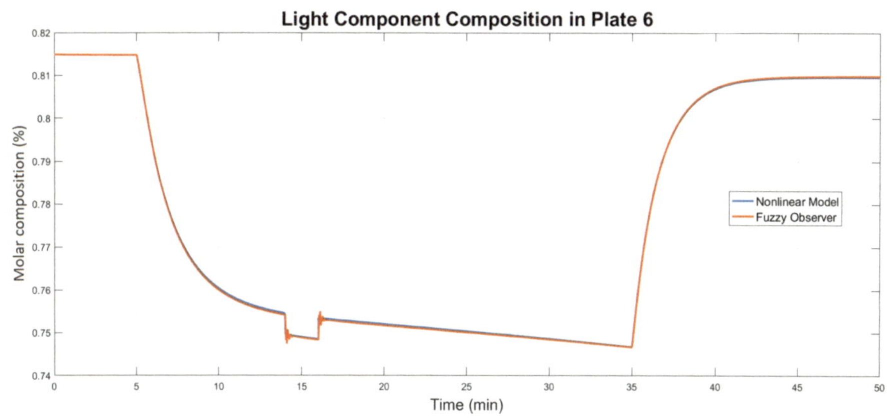

Figure 7.
Plate 6 light component estimation comparison.

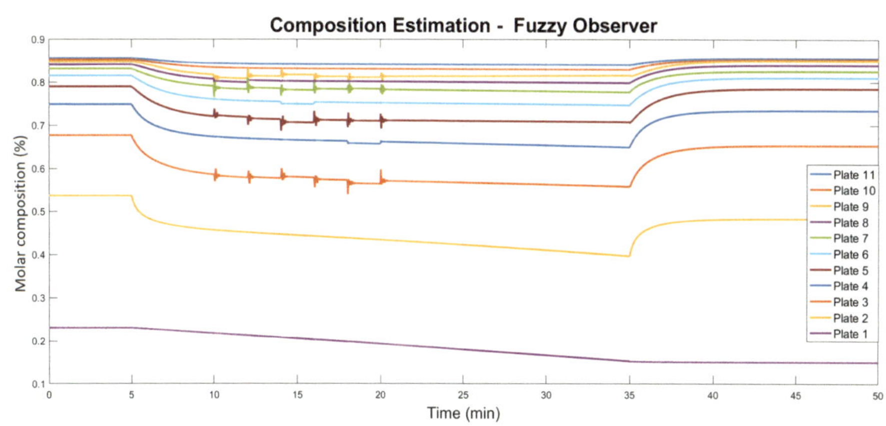

Figure 8.
Plates 4, 6, and 8 light component estimations under disturbances.

It can be noted that the light component composition estimation has a minimum error compared with the composition obtained from the nonlinear model using real data; besides, the convergence time is suitable for an online failure detection system or different control tasks.

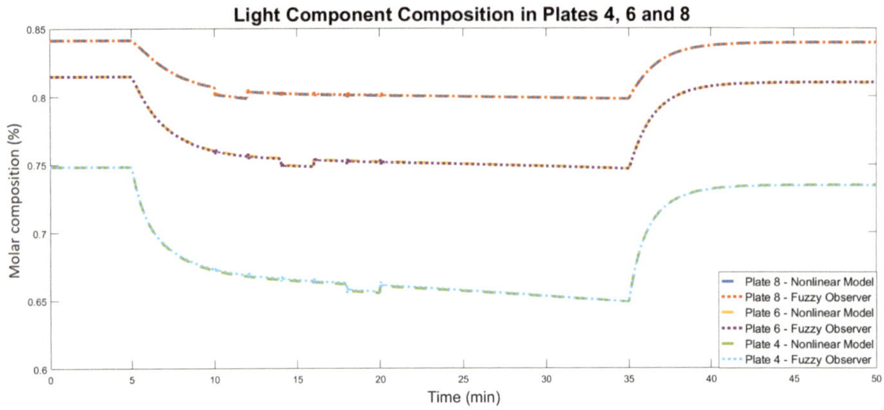

Figure 9.
Plates 4, 6, and 8 light component estimation comparison.

5. Conclusions

In this work a fuzzy observer to estimate the molar composition of the light component in each plate of a binary distillation column is presented. The observer is based on a Takagi-Sugeno fuzzy model of eight rules, taking as premise variables the light component composition in the condenser and in the boiler, as well as the reflux signal.

The gains are calculated by means of LMIs in order to guarantee the stability for each of the closed loop linear subsystems.

The fuzzy observer is validated in simulation by using real data from an 11-plate binary distillation column for an ethanol-water mixture, considering seven RTD temperature sensors and a 300-watt heating resistor. In order to validate the fuzzy observer convergence, different tests were carried out with ideal and different initial conditions between the nonlinear system and the fuzzy observer, as well as disturbances in the light component composition in the nonlinear system.

The observer under different initial conditions has a convergence time of 45 sec. It is also shown that the observer's convergence time under disturbances in the composition of the plate 1 is 1 sec.

Applying from two to seven perturbations to the nonlinear system, it is demonstrated that the observer is robust under multiple perturbations, enabling its implementation as a residual generator in a fault detection system.

Author details

Mario Heras-Cervantes[1], Gerardo Marx Chávez-Campos[2], Héctor Javier Vergara Hernández[2], Adriana del Carmen Téllez-Anguiano[2*], Juan Anzurez-Marin[1] and Elisa Espinosa-Juárez[1]

1 UMSNH, DEPFIE, Morelia, Michoacán, México

2 TecNM/IT Morelia, Morelia, Michoacán, México

*Address all correspondence to: actelleza@gmail.com

References

[1] Ibrahim D, Jobson M, Li J, Guilln Goslbez G. Optimization based design of crude oil distillation units using surrogate column models and a support vector machine. Chemical Engineering Research and Design. 2018;**134**:212-225

[2] Skogestad S. Dynamics and control of distillation columns: A tutorial. Chemical Engineering Research and Design. 1997;**75**(6):539-562

[3] Cingara A, Jovanovic M, Mitrovic M. Analytical first-order dynamic model of binary distillation column. Chemical Engineering. 1990;**45**(12):3585-3592

[4] Kienle A. Low-order dynamic models for ideal multicomponent distillation processes using nonlinear wave propagation theory. Chemical Engineering Science. 2000;**55**(10): 1817-1828

[5] Balasubramhanya LS, Doyle FJ Iii. Nonlinear model-based control of a batch reactive distillation column. Journal of Process Control. 2000;**10**(2): 209-218

[6] Osuolale FN, Zhang J. Energy efficiency optimisation for distillation column using artificial neural network models. Energy. 2016;**106**:562-578

[7] Singh AK, Singh HP, Mishra S. Validation of ann-based model for binary distillation column. In: Proceeding of International Conference on Intelligent Communication, Control and Devices. Singapore: Springer; 2017. pp. 235-242

[8] Lopez-Saucedo ES, Grossmann IE, Segovia-Hernández JG, Hernández S. Rigorous modeling, simulation and optimization of a conventional and nonconventional batch reactive distillation column: A comparative study of dynamic optimization approaches. Chemical Engineering Research and Design. 2016;**111**:83-99

[9] Sree Latha Chopparapu VI, George IT, Bhat VS. Design and simulation of kalman filter for the estimation of tray temperatures in a binary distillation column. International Journal of Pure and Applied Mathematics. 2017;**114**(9): 11-18

[10] Hammouri H, Targui B, Armanet F. High gain observer based on a triangular structure. International Journal of Robust and Nonlinear Control. 2002; **12**(6):497-518

[11] Cervantes MH, Anguiano ACT, Ramrez MCG, Zaragoza CMA, Archundia ER. Validación experimental de un observador de alta ganancia reconfigurable para una columna de destilación. Revista Iberoamericana de Automtica e Informtica Industrial RIAI. 2015;**12**(4):397-407

[12] Astorga CM, Quintero-Marmol E, Vela LG, Torres L. Observador no lineal para la estimación de concentraciones en un proceso de destilación metanol/ etanol. Información tecnológica. 2006; **17**(6):35-41

[13] López-Estrada FR, Ponsart JC, Astorga-Zaragoza CM, Camas-Anzueto JL, Theilliol D. Robust sensor fault estimation for descriptor-LPV systems with unmeasurable gain scheduling functions: Application to an anaerobic bioreactor. International Journal of Applied Mathematics and Computer Science. 2015;**25**(2):233-244

[14] Quintero-Marmol E, Luyben WL, Georgakis C. Application of an extended Luenberger observer to the control of multicomponent batch distillation. Industrial & Engineering Chemistry Research. 1991;**30**(8):1870-1880

[15] Lang L, Gilles ED. Nonlinear observers for distillation columns. Computers & Chemical Engineering. 1990;**14**(11):1297-1301

[16] Zhu Y. Distillation column identification for control using Wiener model. IEEE. 1999;**5**:3462-3466

[17] Safdarnejad M, Gallacher JR, Hedengren JD. Dynamic parameter estimation and optimization for batch distillation. Computers and Chemical Engineering. 2016;**86**:18-32

[18] Angelov PP, Filev DP. An approach to online identification of Takagi-Sugeno fuzzy models. IEEE Transactions on Systems, Man, and Cybernetics, Part B (Cybernetics). 2004;**34**(1):484-498

[19] Takagi T, Sugeno M. Fuzzy Identification of Systems and its Applications to Modeling and Control. IEEE transactions on systems, man, and cybernetics. IEEE. 1985;**1**:116-132

[20] Wang HO, Tanaka K, Griffin M. Parallel distributed compensation of nonlinear systems by takagi-sugeno fuzzy model. IEEE. 1992;**2**:531-538

[21] Sanandaji BM, Salahshoor K, Fatehi A. Multivariable GA-based identification of TS fuzzy models: MIMO distillation column model case study. In: de n Fuzzy Systems Conference, 2007. FUZZ-IEEE 2007; 2007

[22] Sivakumar R, Balu K. ANFIS based distillation column control. In International Journal of Computer Applications Special issue on Evolutionary Computation. 2010;**2**:67-73

[23] Mishra P, Kumar V, Rana KPS. A fractional order fuzzy PID controller for binary distillation column control. Expert Systems with Applications. 2015; **42**(22):8533-8549

[24] Tanaka K, Sugeno M. Stability analysis and design of fuzzy control systems. Fuzzy Sets and Systems. 2004; **45**(2):135-156

[25] Tanaka K, Ikeda T, Wang HO. Fuzzy regulators and fuzzy observers: Relaxed stability conditions and LMI-based designs. IEEE Transactions on Fuzzy Systems. 1998;**6**(2):250-265

[26] Cao Y-Y, Frank PM. Analysis and synthesis of nonlinear time-delay systems via fuzzy control approach. IEEE Transactions on Fuzzy Systems. 2000;**8**(2):200-211

Chapter 3

The Mathematical Model of Basin-Type Solar Distillation Systems

Nguyen The Bao

Abstract

This chapter presents a numerical model for calculating basin-type solar water distillation. The model is used to calculate solar distillation for both passive natural convection and forced convection with external condensers. For passive systems, the numerical model allows to simulate and calculate more complex parameters than previous models. For active-forced convection systems, this model allows the simulations of the heat transfer and mass process inside both the distillation unit and the internal heat exchanger. Comparison of numerical simulation results and experimental results shows that the numerical model achieves the acceptable accuracy in calculating the parameters of the fluid flow inside the distillation and the condenser-type heat recovery as well as estimation of the distillate output corresponding to both types of solar distillation.

Keywords: basin-type solar distillation system, passive solar still, active solar still, forced circulation distillation system with external condenser, enhanced heat recovery

1. Introduction

People in the world are increasingly facing the lack of clean water for living nowadays. Every year, millions of people die from lack of clean water and from the diseases relating to drinking and living water. There is a lot of technology in the world to produce fresh water from sea water or brackish water. However, these technologies are mostly expensive, not suitable for the poor and developing countries and communities where most of the water shortages are occurring. In addition, most of industrial-scale distillation technologies and equipment consume a lot of energy, contributing to the depletion of fossil fuel energy sources and increasing environmental pollution. It is therefore necessary to promote cheap, less energy-efficient, and environmentally friendly distillation methods. The methodology and technology of solar distillation almost meet all three criteria: simple equipment with low-cost, no use of fossil fuels, and no contribution to the environmental pollution.

Solar water distillation is a method of using solar energy, a source of clean and endless energy, to produce clean water from impure water. In solar water distillation equipment, evaporation and purification of pure water occur, thereby removing salts and impurities that are harmful to human health from marine and brackish water resources to give out drinking water. In many solar water distillation technologies and devices, the solar stills are widely used because they are designed and operated in a manner that is consistent with the technological level and economic conditions of the poor and developing countries and communities.

The most popular solar stills are passive type, in which distillation process occurs within the still through evaporation and condensation [1]. They are simple in design and manufacture, easy to operate, usually small, and reasonably cheap. Passive solar stills only use solar energy to remove the salts or impurities in saline or brackish water; thus, it is environmentally friendly and saving energy. Therefore, it is still of value to study in this type of stills to continue improving its efficiencies and designs. This is the main aim of this chapter.

The main drawback of this type of solar distillation system is low energy efficiency and distillate productivities. Hence, many active distillation systems such as solar still coupled with flat plate or evacuated tube collectors, solar still coupled with parabolic concentrator, solar still coupled with heat pipe, solar still coupled with hybrid PV/T system, multistage active solar distillation system, multi-effect active solar distillation system, etc. have been developed theoretically and experimentally [2]. However, a forced circulation solar still with enhanced water recovery has not been researched and presented. Therefore, this type of solar still has been developed and modeled, both theoretically and experimentally, and will be presented in this chapter as well.

In terms of numerical analyses of passive and active solar distillation systems, there are several models presented in literatures [2–8]. Sampathkumar et al. [2] comprehensively reviewed mathematical models applied to predict the performances of active solar distillation systems and concluded that Kumar and Tiwari's model [3] was most suitable for evaluating the internal heat transfer coefficients and hourly yield accurately except in extreme cases. However, Dwivedi and Tiwari [4] observed from their studies in passive solar still that Dunkle's model [5] gave better agreement between theoretical and experimental results. Madhlopa and Johnstone [6] numerically modeled a passive solar still with separate condenser and claimed that the distillation productivity of their still was 62% higher than that of the conventional passive solar still. Ahsan et al. [7] reviewed a few numerical models of a tubular solar still and compared them with Dunkle and Ueda models. Recently, Edalatpour et al. [8] reviewed the latest developments in numerical simulations for solar stills including the use of computational fluid dynamics (CFD) simulations, MATLAB.

Based on the above literature review, it is obvious that although Dunkle's model is one of the oldest thermal model for predicting the internal heat transfers of solar stills, it still can be used to accurately present the performance of heat transfers inside the solar stills. However, there is no research found in the literature review that consistently uses Dunkle's equations to develop the numerical models for both passive and active solar stills. Therefore, this chapter will use this approach to develop the mathematical models for a conventional solar still and a forced circulation solar still with enhanced water recovery.

2. The mathematical model of a passive basin-type solar still

The relationships of heat and mass transfer in a solar still under steady-state conditions were first studied in 1961 by Dunkle [5]. Based on this initial work, this research has developed the transient mode of the solar still in which all heat and mass coefficients and still parameters are calculated using the formulae within the model. The weather data used for simulation will be either input from actual measured data or data generated from a sub-computer program developed by the author and linked to the main program [9].

The processes of heat and mass transfer in a passive solar still are indicated in **Figure 1**. In order to develop the formulae for the energy and mass balances in the still, the following assumptions are made:

- The lost amount of water through evaporation is small compared to the amount of water in the basin and can be ignored.
- The energy required to heat up the water from outside temperature before adding to the still to the basin temperature is negligible as compared to the latent energy required to evaporate the same amount of water. In other words, $C_{pw}(T_w - T_a) \ll h_w$.
- There is no leakage in a well-designed still.
- The areas of the cover, the water surface, and the still basin are equal.
- The temperature gradients along the cover thickness and the water depth are ignored.

As can be seen in **Figure 1**, the heat and mass transfer inside the solar still occurs as follows: the solar incidence Q_T from the sun reaches the glass, part of it will be reflected Q_r, part will be absorbed by the glass Q_α, and the remaining Q' will transfer through the glass and reach the basin water. Then, Q' absorbed into the basin water will be partially reflected back to the glass under convection q_{cw}, evaporation q_{ew}, and radiation q_{rw}, partially transfer to the basin $q_{w\text{-}b}$, and the remaining will increase the temperature of the basin water $M_w \frac{dT_w}{dt}$. The basin, in its turn, gains the energy partially from the sun $(\alpha Q_T'')$, partially from the water $(q_{w\text{-}b})$.

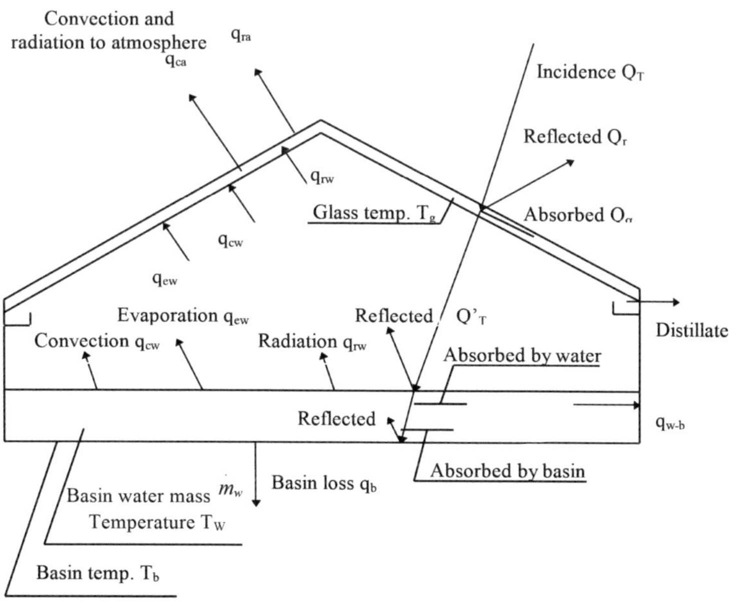

Figure 1.
The heat and mass transfer processes in a conventional solar still.

This gained energy will be partially lost from surroundings q_b, and the remaining will increase the temperature of the basin $M_b \frac{dT_b}{dt}$. Similarly, the energy going in the glass includes the reflected energy from the basin water through convection q_{cw}, evaporation q_{ew}, radiation q_{rw}, and the energy absorbed from the sun $\alpha_g Q_T$. This gained energy of the glass will partially transfer to the ambient through convection q_{ca} and radiation q_{ra} and partially increase the temperature of the glass $M_g \frac{dT_g}{dt}$.

Based on these assumptions and the heat and mass transfer explained above, the energy balances for the glass, for the basin water and for the basin, are

$$q_{cw} + q_{ew} + q_{rw} + \alpha_g Q_T = (q_{ra} + q_{ca}) + M_g \frac{dT_g}{dt} \tag{1}$$

$$\alpha_w Q_T' = q_{cw} + q_{ew} + q_{rw} + q_{w-b} + M_w \frac{dT_w}{dt} \tag{2}$$

$$\alpha_b Q_T'' + q_{w-b} = q_b + M_b \frac{dT_b}{dt} \tag{3}$$

where

q_{cw}: heat transfer by convection from the still water to the glass (W/m^2), which is calculated by using Dunkle's equation:

$$q_{cw} = 0.884 \left[(T_w - T_g) + \frac{(p_w - p_g)(T_w + 273)}{(268.9 \times 10^3 - p_w)} \right]^{1/3} (T_w - T_g) \tag{4}$$

with p_w and p_g being the partial pressure of water vapor at the temperatures of the basin water and the glass, respectively (in Pa).

q_{ew}: heat transfer by evaporation from the still water to the glass (W/m^2):

$$q_{ew} = 16.276 \times 10^{-3} q_{cw} \frac{(p_w - p_g)}{(T_w - T_g)} \tag{5}$$

q_{rw}: heat transfer by radiation from the basin water to the glass cover (W/m^2), given by

$$q_{rw} = \varepsilon_w \sigma \left[(T_w + 273)^4 - (T_g + 273)^4 \right] \tag{6}$$

where ε_w is the emission of water

$$\sigma = 5.67 \times 10^{-8} \mathrm{W/m^2.K^4}$$

q_{ca}: heat transfer by convection from the glass to the ambient around the still (W/m^2), calculated as [10]

$$q_{ca} = (5.7_w + 3.8)(T_g - T_a) \tag{7}$$

with $\mathcal{W}$ being the velocity of wind (m/s) and T_a the temperature of the atmosphere (°C).

q_{ra}: *heat* transfer by radiation from the glass to the ambient around the still (W/m^2):

$$q_{ra} = \varepsilon_g \sigma \left[(T_g + 273)^4 - (T_a + 273)^4 \right] \tag{8}$$

where ε_g is the emission of the glass.

q_{w-b}: heat transfer by convection from the still water to the absorbing surface of the basin (W/m^2):

$$q_{w-b} = h_{w-b}(T_w - T_b) \tag{9}$$

where h_{w-b} is the coefficient of convection from the water to the basin ($W/m^2.°C$).

q_b: heat transfer by convection from the basin to the surroundings of the still (W/m^2):

$$q_b = h_b(T_b - T_a) \tag{10}$$

where h_b is the coefficient of convection from the basin to the ambient around the still ($W/m^2.°C$):

$$\frac{1}{h_b} = \frac{\delta_{insul}}{k_{insul}} + \frac{1}{h_i} \tag{11}$$

k_{insul} (W/m.°C) and δ_{insul} (m) are the basin thermal conductivity and the thickness of the basin insulation, respectively.

h_i: the combination of heat transfer coefficients by convection and radiation from the basin insulation to the ambient surroundings, which can be derived from formulae (6) and (7).

Q_T: global solar irradiation to the cover, in W/m^2.

Q'_T: global solar irradiation dropping on the still water, after transmitting through the glass, in W/m^2.

Q''_T: global solar irradiation dropping on the basin, after transmitting through the still water, in W/m^2.

α_b, α_w, and α_g: solar radiation absorption coefficients of the basin, water, and glass, respectively.

M_b, M_w, and M_g: solar radiation heat capacities per unit area of the basin, water, and glass, in $J/m^2.°C$.

T_b, T_w, and T_g: transient temperatures of the basin, of the water, and of the glass, respectively, in °C.

Formulae (1), (2), and (3) can be derived as follows:

$$M_g \frac{dT_g}{dt} = \propto_g Q_T + q_{cw} + q_{ew} + q_{rw} - (q_{ra} + q_{ca}) \tag{12}$$

$$M_w \frac{dT_w}{dt} = \propto_w Q'_T - (q_{cw} + q_{ew} + q_{rw} + q_{w-b}) \tag{13}$$

$$M_b \frac{dT_b}{dt} = \propto_b Q''_T + q_{w-b} - q_b \tag{14}$$

It is often to present all solar components Q_T, Q_T', and Q_T'' in the above formulae by the global solar incidence of the sloped cover, Q_T, which is well-known computed [9]. If τ_b, τ_w, and τ_g are, respectively, defined as the proportions of solar radiation incident absorbed by the basin, water, and glass liner, formulae (12), (13), and (14) can be written as

$$M_g \frac{dT_g}{dt} = \tau_b Q_T + q_{cw} + q_{ew} + q_{rw} - \left(q_{ra} + q_{ca}\right) \quad (15)$$

$$M_w \frac{dT_w}{dt} = \tau_w Q_T - \left(q_{cw} + q_{ew} + q_{rw} + q_{w-b}\right) \quad (16)$$

$$M_b \frac{dT_b}{dt} = \tau_b Q_T + q_{w-b} - q_b \quad (17)$$

3. The mathematical model of an active basin-type solar distillation system with enhanced water recovery condenser

This section will focus in developing the relationships of heat and mass transfer in an active solar distillation system with enhanced water recovery condenser. Then, this mathematical model will be validated by comparing its results with those from the experimental model.

An active solar distillation system with enhanced water recovery condenser has been chosen in this study for several reasons. Compared with other types of active solar stills such as solar stills coupled with flat plate or evacuated tube collectors, solar stills coupled with parabolic concentrator, solar stills coupled with heat pipe, solar stills coupled with hybrid PV/T system, multistage active solar distillation systems, multi-effect active solar distillation systems, etc., solar stills represent simple yet mature technology. This is suitable for poor and developing countries and communities like Vietnam.

The main disadvantage of a conventional passive solar still as low productivity and efficiency can be overcome by changing the principle of operation as follows:

- Using air as an intermediate fluid and using forced convection to increase the heat transfer in the still, leading to increase the evaporation of water.

- Replacing saturated air in the passive solar still by "drier" air to increase the potential for mass transfer in the still, resulting in increasing the distillate outputs.

- Circulating the air-vapor mixture from the passive still to an external condenser to increase efficiency from a lower condensing temperature. If the water with low temperatures such as well water or wastewater from refrigeration process is available, then this condensing process will be more effective.

- Recovering heat extracted in the condensing process and using it to preheat the air-vapor mixture entering the still.

- Replacing the limited condensing area of the hot glass covers in the standard still by the external condenser with much larger heat exchange areas and much lower temperature to increase condensing process.

3.1 Developing of the relationships of heat and mass transfer in an active solar distillation system

Figure 2 presents a schematic diagram of an active solar distillation system with enhanced water recovery condenser. The airflow entering the solar still with a temperature of T_{fin} and moisture content w_{in} is heated up. After absorbing the vapor from the basin water, the airflow exits the solar still at a temperature of T_{fout} and moisture content w_{out}. Then the hot air-vapor mixture passes through the dehumidifying coil, acting as a condenser. The dehumidifying coil with cooling water running inside will cool the hot air-vapor mixture down and condense the vapor from the mixture to produce the distillate. The air after passing the condenser has $T_{c\text{-}out}$ and $w_{c\text{-}out}$. The airflow continues passing through the preheater before going back to the still; hence, part of its heat will be extracted to recover in the preheater.

The heat and mass transfer relationships in this still can be seen in **Figure 3**. The heat and mass transfer is mainly similar to that of the conventional solar still, except the energy reflecting from the basin water through convection q_{cw} and evaporation q_{ew} will go into the flowing air first (defined as q_{cwf} and q_{ew}) instead of going directly to glass as in the conventional case. Then, the flowing air (the flow) will release part of its energy to the glass through convection q_{cfg}. The gained energy of the flow, mainly from the basin water, will increase both latent heat $(h_{out} - h_{in})$ and sensible heat $M_f \frac{dT_f}{dt}$ of the flow.

From **Figure 3**, the energy and mass balances for the glass, for the flow in the still, for the basin water, and for the basin are

$$q_{cfg} + q_{rw} + \alpha_g Q_T = (q_{ra} + q_{ca}) + M_g \frac{dT_g}{dt} \tag{18}$$

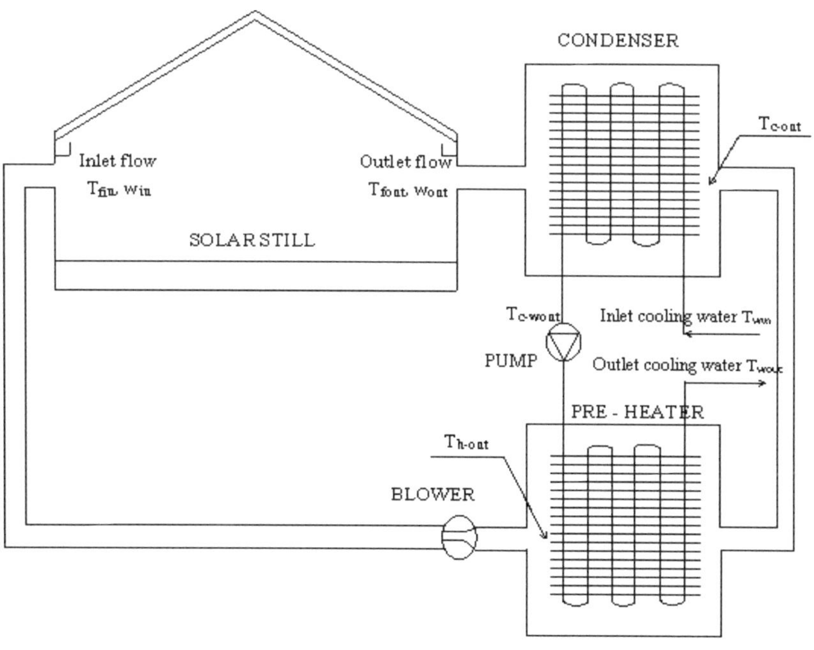

Figure 2.
Schematic diagram of a forced circulation solar still with enhanced water recovery.

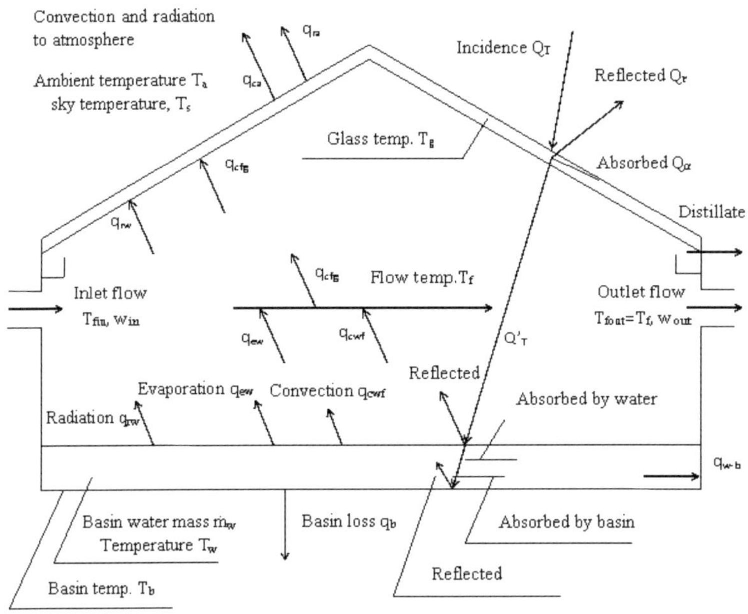

Figure 3.
The heat and mass transfer process in a forced circulation solar still.

$$q_{ew} + q_{cwf} = q_{cfg} + m_f(h_{out} - h) + M_f \frac{dT_f}{dt} \tag{19}$$

$$m_{ew} = \frac{q_{ew}}{h_{fg}} = m_f(w_{out} - w) + m_{ew-g} \tag{20}$$

$$\alpha_w Q'_T = q_{cwf} + q_{ew} + q_{rw} + q_{w-b} + M_w \frac{dT_w}{dt} \tag{21}$$

$$\alpha_b Q''_T + q_{w-b} = q_b + M_b \frac{dT_b}{dt} \tag{22}$$

q_{cwf}: heat transfer by convection from the still water to the air (W/m^2). In theory, the blower flowing the air must use energy as low as possible, or it should be powered by solar PV system. Depending on the flow velocity, the process of heat transfer in the still may be in natural or forced mode. Therefore, in this mathematical model, the coefficient of heat transfer in the still is computed by using both Reynolds and Grashof numbers for the forced and natural convection relations separately; then the larger one is chosen [10]:

$$Gr = \frac{g\beta' \Delta T L^3}{\nu^2} \tag{23}$$

$$Re = \frac{VD_h}{\nu} \tag{24}$$

where L is the distance between the water surface and the glass, in m; g = 9.81 m/s^2 is the gravity constant; β' is the volumetric expansion coefficient, in K^{-1}; for air $\beta' = 1/T$; ΔT is the difference between the water and the glass temperatures, in ^{0}C; ν is the kinematic viscosity, in m/s^2; V is the airflow velocity, in m/s; $D_h = \frac{4(flow\ area)}{wetted\ perimeter}$ is the hydraulic diameter of the solar still.

If the natural mode dominates, the heat transfer by convection from the still water to the airflow can be calculated from

$$Nu = \frac{h_{cwf}L}{k} = 0.075(Gr.Pr)^{1/3} \tag{25}$$

with $Pr = \frac{\nu}{\alpha}$ being the Prandtl number.

In order to have the same format with Dunkle's expression [11], T_f is replaced for T_g:

$$q_{cwf} = 0.884\left[(T_w - T_f) + \frac{(T_w - T_f)(T_w + 273.15)}{(268 \times 10^3 - p_w)}\right]^{1/3}(T_w - T_f) \tag{26}$$

where p_f and p_w are, respectively, the partial water vapor pressures at the temperatures of the flow and the basin water, in Pa.

If the forced convection dominates, the relation between Nu and Re is given by [10]

$$Nu = \frac{h_{cwf}D_h}{k} = 0.664 \times Re^{1/2} \times Pr^{1/3} \tag{27}$$

Considering T_w = 50°C and T_f = 40°C and introducing the corresponding air properties into Eq. (27), the convective heat transfer rate between the basin water and the flow can be computed by

$$q_{cwf} = 3.91\left(\frac{V}{D_h}\right)^{1/2}(T_W - T_f) \tag{28}$$

q_{ew}: heat transfer by evaporation (W/m^2) from the still water to the flow, which is calculated using formula (5) with p_f and T_f are replaced for p_g and T_g.

q_{rw}: heat transfer by radiation (W/m^2) from the still water to the glass, which is computed by using formula (6).

q_{cfg}: heat transfer by convection (W/m^2) from the air to the glass, which is computed as

$$q_{cfg} = 2.8\left(\frac{V^{4/5}}{L_s^{1/5}}\right)(T_f - T_g) \tag{29}$$

with V the airflow velocity (m/s) and L_s are the still length (m).

q_{ca} and q_{ra} are, respectively, the heat transfer rates by convection and radiation (W/m^2) from the glass and the ambient around the still, calculated from formulae (7) and (8) correspondently.

$q_{w\text{-}b}$ and q_b are the heat transfer (W/m^2) from the still water to the basin and from the basin to the ambient around the still and computed from formulae (9) and (10) correspondently.

Q_T: the global solar irradiation dropping on the still (W/m^2).

Q'_T: the global solar irradiation dropping on the water, after transmitting through the glass, (W/m^2).

Q''_T: global solar irradiation dropping on the basin, after transmitting through the still water, (W/m^2).

m_f: the airflow mass rate, in kg/s.

m_{ew}: the mass rate evaporating from the basin water to the airflow, in kg/s.

α_b, α_w,and α_g: solar absorption ratios of the basin, of the water and of the glass correspondently.

M_b, M_f, M_w, and M_g: heat mass are unit area of the basin, the air, the water in the still, and the glass (J/m^2.°C).

T_b, T_f, T_w, and T_g: respectively, the basin, the airflow, the still water, and the glass temperatures (°C).

h_{fg}: latent heat of vaporization of water at T_f (J/kg).

w_{out} and w_{in}: the air-vapor mixture's moisture contents exit and enter the still (kg/kg).

h_{out} and h_{in}: respectively, the enthalpies of air exiting and entering the still (J/kg). The air enthalpy exiting the still h_{out} can be computed as the temperature T_f function as follows:

$$h_{out} = \left(T_f + w_{out\times}\left(2500 + 1.81T_f\right)\right) \times 10^3 \tag{30}$$

The yield of the distillate in the solar still depends on the air and the glass temperatures. Water will condense on the glass surface only when the airflow dew point temperature T_{fd} is higher than the glass temperature T_g. In this case, the amount of the distillate produced from the glass $m_{ew\text{-}g}$ can be computed from (kg/s m^2):

$$\dot{m}_{ew-g} = \frac{q_{con-g}}{h_{fg}} \tag{31}$$

h_{fg}: latent heat of vaporization of water at T_f, (J/kg).

$q_{con\text{-}g} = h_{con\text{-}g}(T_f - T_g)$: heat transfer by condensation from the airflow to the glass. Using the Nusselt to calculate

$$Nu = \frac{h_{con-g}L_c}{k} = 0.943\left(\frac{g^2 sin\beta h_{fg}L_c^3}{\mu k\Delta T}\right)^{1/4} \tag{32}$$

where L_c is the length of the glass, in m; $L_c = L_s$; k is the thermal conductivity, in W/m K; g = 9.81 m/s^2 gravity constant; β is the slope of the glass, in degree; ρ is the air density, in kg/m^3; ΔT is the dew point temperature difference between the airflow and the glass, in °K; μ is absolute viscosity, in Pa s.

Using the properties of the air at T_f = 40°C, one can achieve

$$q_{con-g} = 70.93\left(\frac{sin\beta}{\Delta TL_c}\right)^{0.25} \tag{33}$$

Hence, with five formulae from (18) to (19), five parameters T_g, T_w, T_f, w_{out}, and T_b, can be found.

3.2 The dehumidifying coil and preheating coil calculation

The calculation of dehumidifying and preheating coils has been studied and is shown in [11, 12]. However, a clear and detailed procedure for simulating the performance of dehumidifying coils was not available in these references. Hence, a numerical model of the performance of the dehumidifying and the preheater coils in this research was developed from the handbook and the standard. The calculation procedures for the psychometric properties of humid air were given in [11]. A detailed procedure for simulating the coils of preheating and dehumidifying of an active distillation system is presented in [9].

The simulation of the preheater includes (i) computing the heat transfer coefficient for the coil, (ii) computing the coil effectiveness, and then (iii) calculating the air and cooling water temperatures leaving the coil.

The simulation of the dehumidifying includes finding consistent values of temperature and humidity by using an iterative process.

4. The comparison of results from numerical modeling and experimental results

4.1 The passive solar still

Figures 4 and **5** show the computed distillate yields and still water temperatures from the mathematical model compared to those from the experiments. As shown in these figures, the simulation model developed in this study gave very accurate calculated results. Hence, one can confidently use this program to simulate solar passive stills.

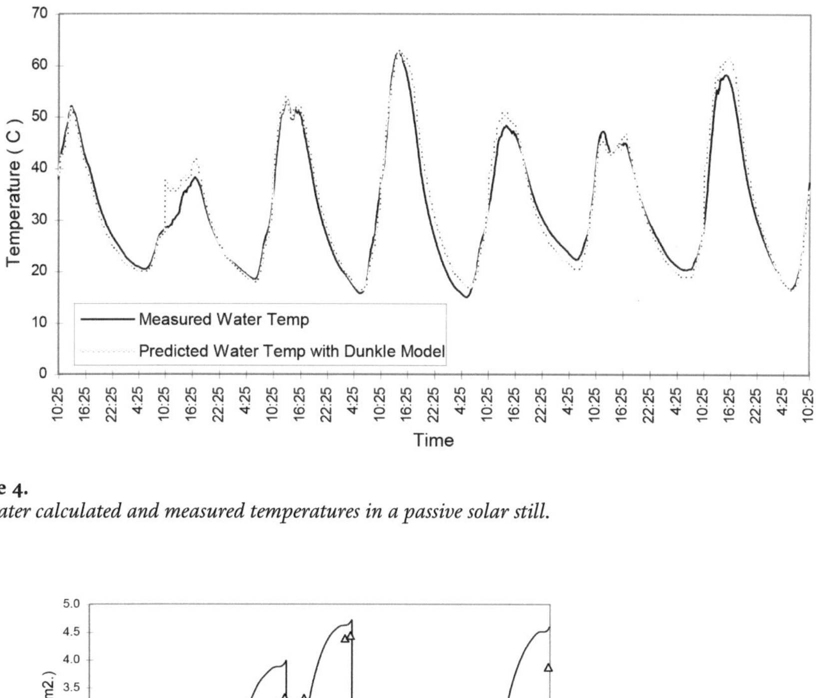

Figure 4.
The water calculated and measured temperatures in a passive solar still.

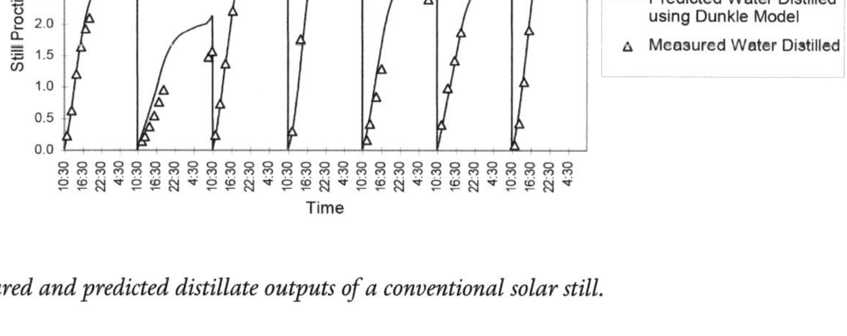

Figure 5.
The measured and predicted distillate outputs of a conventional solar still.

4.2 The active solar distillation system with external condenser and enhanced water recovery

To simulate the performance of the active distillation system, the computer program is first input with the measured weather parameters of the site and the measured values of the air entering the still's relative humidity and temperature. The results of the simulation program include still water temperature, glass temperature, basin temperature, air leaving the still temperature and relative humidity, air leaving the condenser temperature, and air leaving heat recovery's temperature and relative humidity, as well as the distillate production from the glass and from the condenser. **Figure 6** shows the measured and predicted temperatures and relative humidity of the air leaving the still, while **Figure 7** shows those of the air leaving the preheater. **Figure 8** shows the air leaving the still calculated and measured moisture content, and **Figure 9** shows the basin water calculated and measured temperatures. **Figures 10** and **11** correspondingly show the calculated and measured distillate yields from the glass and the condenser.

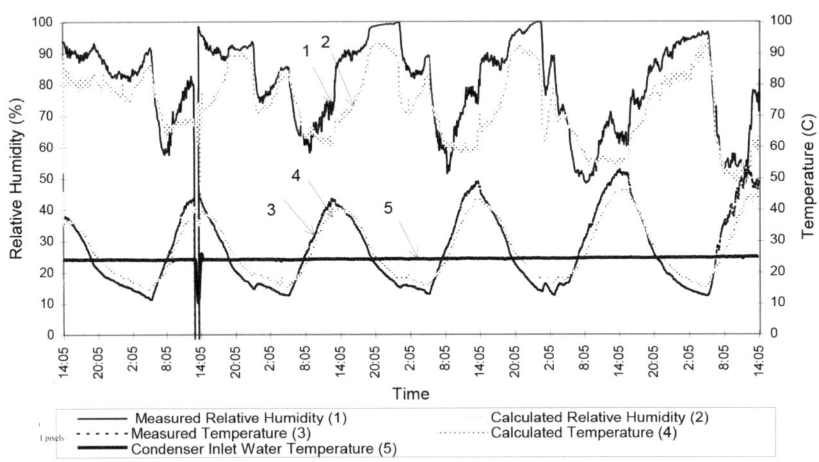

Figure 6.
The predicted and measured temperature and relative humidity of the air leaving the forced convection still.

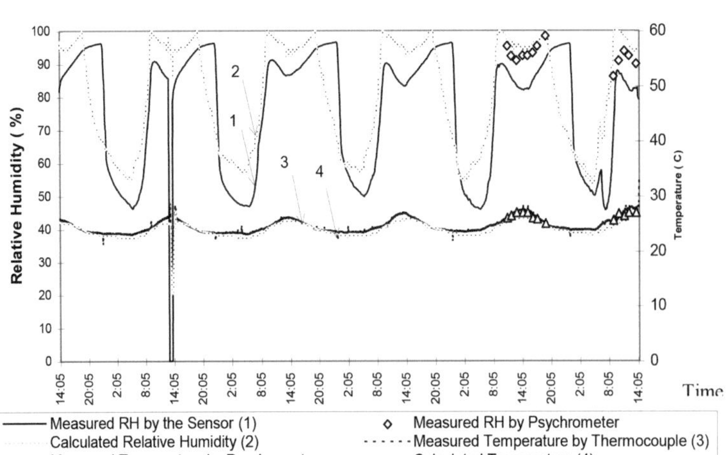

Figure 7.
The predicted and measured temperature and relative humidity of the air leaving the preheater.

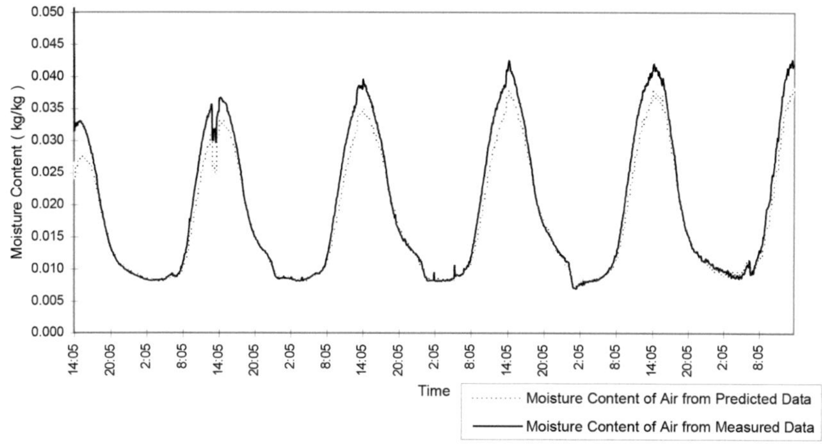

Figure 8.
The predicted and measured moisture content of the air leaving the still.

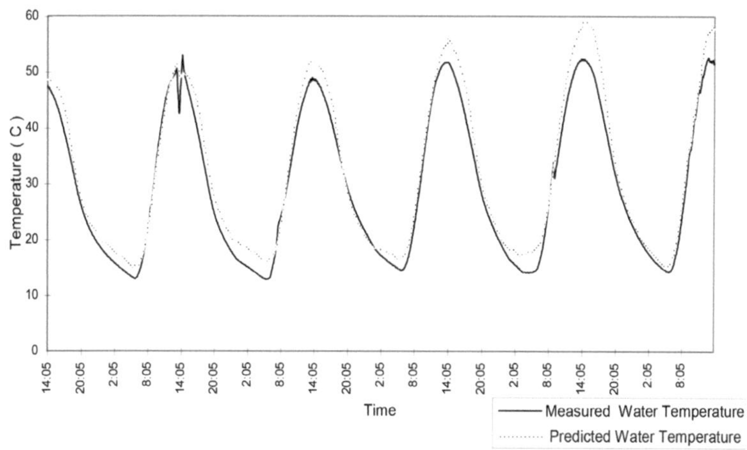

Figure 9.
The predicted and measured temperature of the water in the still.

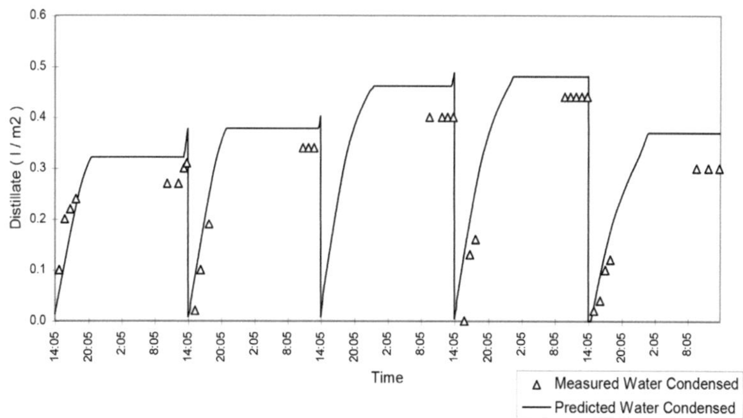

Figure 10.
The predicted and measured distillate condensed on the glass of the still.

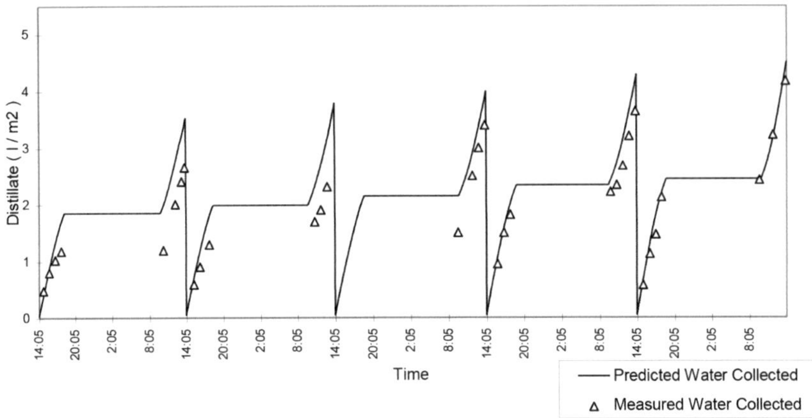

Figure 11.
The predicted and measured distillate collected from the condenser of the still.

As shown in **Figure 6**, the mathematical model can predict reasonably well both the actual values and the trend of the temperature of the air leaving the still. The maximum error of the calculated temperatures compared to measured values is 5°C and occurs in the early afternoon. The average errors in the relative humidity calculation are around 10% with maximum error values up to 20%. In most cases, the computed values are lower than the measured ones. **Figure 8** once again confirms that the mathematical model underestimates the moisture in the air leaving the still in the middle of the day. At other times, the predicted and measured computed moisture contents of the outlet air are similar, which shows the observed variations in relative humidity at these times are due to difference between the predicted and measured air temperatures.

5. Conclusion

In this chapter, a numerical model for calculating basin-type solar water distillation was presented. The model can be used to calculate solar distillation for both passive natural convection and forced convection with external condensers. For passive systems, the numerical model allows to simulate and calculate more complex parameters than previous models. For active-forced convection systems, this model allows the simulations of the heat transfer and mass process inside both the distillation unit and the internal heat exchanger. Comparison of numerical simulation results and experimental results showed that the numerical model achieves the acceptable accuracy in calculating the parameters of the fluid flow inside the distillation and the condenser-type heat recovery as well as estimation of the distillate output corresponding to both types of solar distillation.

Author details

Nguyen The Bao
Department of Heat and Refrigeration Engineering, Faculty of Mechanical Engineering, University of Technology, Vietnam National University of Ho Chi Minh City, Ho Chi Minh City, Vietnam

*Address all correspondence to: drthebao@gmail.com

References

[1] Manchanda H, Kumar M. A comprehensive decade review and analysis on designs and performance parameters of passive solar still. Renewables: Wind, Water and Solar, Springer Open Journal. 2015;(2):1-24. DOI: 10.1186/s40807-015-0019-8

[2] Sampathkumar K, Arjunan TV, Pitchandi P, Senthilkumar P. Active solar distillation—A detailed review. Renewable and Sustainable Energy Reviews. 2010;**14**:1503-1526

[3] Kumar S, Tiwari GN. Estimation of convective mass transfer in solar distillation systems. Solar Energy. 1996; **57**(6):459-464

[4] Dwivedi VK, Tiwari GN. Experimental validation of thermal model of a double slope active solar still under natural circulation mode. Desalination. 2010;**250**:49-55

[5] Dunkle RV. Solar water distillation: The roof type still and a multiple effect diffusion still. International Developments in Heat Transfer, American Society of Mechanical Engineers, Proceedings of International Heat Transfer, Part V. University of Colorado. 1961. pp. 895-902

[6] Madhlopa A, Johnstone C. Numerical study of a passive solar still with separate condenser. Renewable Energy. 2009;**34**(7):1668-1677

[7] Ahsan A, Imteaz M, Dev R, Arafat HA. Numerical models of solar distillation device: Present and previous. Desalination. 2013;**311**:173-181

[8] Edalatpour M, Aryna K, Kianifar A, Tiwari GN, Mahian O, Wongwises S. Solar stills: A review of the latest developments in numerical simulations. Solar Energy. 2016;**135**:897-922

[9] Bao NT. SOLSTILL—A simulation program for solar distillation systems. In: Proceedings of EUROSUN 2004; Freiburg, Germany. 2004. pp. 96-105

[10] Duffie JA, Beckman WA. Solar Engineering of Thermal Processes. 4th ed. New York: John Wiley and Sons Inc.; 2013

[11] ASHRAE Systems and Equipment Handbook. New York: American Society of Heating, Refrigerating and Air-Conditioning Engineers; 2012

[12] AHRI. Forced-Circulation Air-Cooling and Heating Coils. Standard 410. Arlington, VA: Air-Conditioning, Heating and Refrigeration Institute; 2014

Section 3

Phase Equilibrium

Chapter 4

A Practical Fitting Method Involving a Trade-Off Decision in the Parametrization Procedure of a Thermodynamic Model and Its Repercussion on Distillation Processes

Adriel Sosa, Luís Fernández, Elena Gómez, Eugénia A. Macedo and Juan Ortega

Abstract

The design of processes containing information on phase equilibria must be carried out through a series of steps, experimentation ↔ verification ↔ modeling ↔ simulation. Each of these steps should be rigorously performed to guarantee a good representation of the behavior of the system under study, whose adequate modeling could be used to simulate the corresponding process. To carry out the different previous tasks, two representative systems, extracted from known database, are used. The quality checking of experimental data series is certified through several thermodynamic consistency methods. The modeling is done by applying a multi-objective optimization procedure, which allows to define a *solution front* (*Pareto front*) for different sub-models that are established in this work. The fitness of trade-off solutions, obtained from the *efficient front*, on the design of distillation processes is analyzed through a simulation.

Keywords: multiproperty modeling, optimization procedure, trade-off decision, distillation, simulation

1. Introduction

Nowadays, process simulation [1] plays an important role in the chemical engineering field as an indispensable tool to gain precise knowledge about the process units. The use of powerful mathematical-computational tools allows to accomplish an optimal final design of chemical processes. An important matter is to ensure that the mathematical model correctly represents the quantities that reflect the state of the studied system. Then, what is a model? A model is a mathematical relationship that links the state variables of a system, such as temperature, pressure, or compositions, influencing the process performance. Therefore, the accuracy of the selected model is essential and greatly affects the final results of the simulation and design processes. Two milestones should be considered.

The first one is the selection of the model, built-in with the mathematical relationships that best represent the variables of the system. There is no a priori a procedure to make this choice, so heuristic or experience-based criteria are generally used [2]. The second question refers to get the best parameters that complete the definition of the model for a given data series. For this latter case, there are several numerical procedures [3, 4] that allow to address the problem to optimize the parameter set considering the starting hypothesis.

The thermodynamic properties having the greatest influence on the simulation of separation processes are those related to phase equilibria (vapor-liquid equilibrium, VLE, in the scope of this work), as well as other thermodynamic quantities that arise in the mixing process. These properties are associated with the excess Gibbs energy g^E, which is written as $g^E = g^E(x_i,p,T)$. As such, the goal of the modeling is to achieve a functional type of $f = f(\boldsymbol{\theta},x_i,p,T)$ that minimizes the norm $|g^E - f|$. The vector $\boldsymbol{\theta}$ represents a set of parameters in the model, which must be optimized. However, due to the existing relation between phase and mixing properties, former approach may not be enough. In the first place, g^E values can only be obtained from VLE, which satisfies a dependency of the type, $F(x_i,p,T) = 0$, preventing us from obtaining individual relations of g^E with each one of the variables. On the other hand, defects in the experimental data could give place to incoherencies between experimental activity coefficients $\gamma_i = \gamma_i(x_i,y_i,p,T)$ and the excess Gibbs function g^E. Thus, the VLE fitting process becomes a bi-objective optimization problem; hence, two error functions are included in the correlation problem. The complexity grows as other properties, such as $h^E = h^E(x,p,T)$, are included in the modeling, since new error functions should also be minimized. However, one of the benefits of this approach is to use a unique thermodynamic model that avoids the issues caused by possible discontinuities or inconsistencies between partial models of some properties. Even more relevant is that this allows the model to describe better the physics of the system under study. This supposes a mean to verify the coherence of the mathematical formalism imposed by thermodynamics, validating the different properties. A drawback of this practice is the increase of the complexity of the procedure, but this is just a numerical issue of relative complexity. Therefore, addressing the global modeling of the thermodynamic behavior of solutions as a problem with multiple objectives is a notable contribution in chemical engineering.

It is known that the resolution of multi-objective problems does not produce a single result; on the contrary, a set of non-dominated results that constitute the so-called Pareto front [5] is obtained. There is no precise mathematical criterion that allows the selection of a unique result. However, the process simulation requires a single result to define the intended design, having to resort to external criteria different from those used to obtain the *front*.

This study evaluates the effect of choosing the different results from the *Pareto front* in the simulation task. To achieve this, some partial goals are proposed such as (a) to establish a rigorous methodology to carry out the optimization procedure with the suggested modeling and (b) to check the real impact of the chosen model on the simulation, with the purpose of proposing a selection criterion. Thus, the designed methodology should include different stages, like the data selection used in the procedure, obtaining the *result front* and the election of the final *result.* Two systems, considered as standard in many studies on thermodynamic behavior of solutions, are selected since the necessary experimental information (VLE and h^E) is available in literature. After checking the data sets [6, 7], making up the *testing* ↔ *modeling* steps, and having obtained the corresponding *result fronts*, each candidate model is analyzed on its suitability for process simulation.

2. Modeling procedures

2.1 Thermodynamic model

The correlation of the iso-p {VLE + h^E} data for each one of the two systems selected is carried out using a parametric equation already used by us [8], which is applied to the excess Gibbs function of a binary system:

$$g^E(p,T,\mathbf{x}) = z_1(1-z_1)\sum_{i=0}^{2} g_i(p,T)z_1^i z_1 = \frac{x_1}{x_1 + k_g^{2\text{-}1} x_2} \tag{1}$$

and as described in [8]:

$$g_i(p,T) = g_{i1} + g_{i2}p^2 + g_{i3}pT + g_{i4}/T + g_{i5}T^2 \tag{2}$$

where k_g^{2-1} is a fitting parameter. In this study, several forms of Eq. (2) are tested, by adapting it according to the availability of experimental data. Thus, different "sub-models" are defined by neglecting terms in Eq. (2) which give rise to the following four cases:

$$\begin{aligned} &\text{M1} \rightarrow \{g_{i2}, g_{i3}, g_{i4}, g_{i5}\} = 0; \text{M2} \rightarrow \{g_{i2}, g_{i3}, g_{i5}\} = 0; \\ &\text{M3} \rightarrow \{g_{i2}, g_{i5}\} = 0; \text{M4} \rightarrow g_{i2} = 0 \end{aligned} \tag{3}$$

From Eq. (1), the expression that characterizes the activity coefficients is

$$\begin{aligned} RT\ln\gamma_i = {} & z_1(1-z_1)\left(g_0 + g_1 z_1 + g_2 z_1^2\right) + (1 - i - x_1) \\ & \left[g_0 + 2(g_1 - g_0)z_1 + 3(g_2 - g_1)z_1^2 - 4g_2 z_1^3\right] k_g^{2\text{-}1}(z_1/x_1)^2 \end{aligned} \tag{4}$$

Likewise, the excess enthalpies h^E are calculated considering.

$$h^E = g^E - T\left(\partial g^E/\partial T\right)_{x,p}; h^E = z_1(1-z_1)\left(h_0 + h_1 z_1 + h_2 z_1^2\right) \tag{5}$$

Eqs. (1) and (5) assume that the different sub-models established by Eq. (3) impose certain behavior hypothesis in the mixture. Thus, sub-model M1 implies that $g^E = h^E$. For the remaining assumptions, $g^E \neq h^E$, allowing different functions to express the h^Es.

2.2 Calculation of the *efficient fronts*

To obtain the optimal parameters of the different sub-models that represent the data set iso-p VLE and h^E, the multi-objective optimization (MOO) procedure is used, which is characterized by the vector

$$\mathbf{OF} = \left[s\left(g^E/RT\right)\ s\left(h^E\right)\right] \tag{6}$$

where $s(y^E)$ is the root of the mean square error (or RMSE) calculated by the model when representing the generic property y^E:

$$s(y^{\mathrm{E}}) = \left[\sum\left(y_{\mathrm{exp}}^{\mathrm{E}} - y_{\mathrm{cal}}^{\mathrm{E}}\right)^2/m\right]^{0.5};m = \text{number of experimental points} \quad (7)$$

The result of such a problem is a discrete set of values, taken from the *efficient front*, $s(g^E/RT) = f[s(h^E)]$, where each one of these give rise to different estimates of the thermodynamic behavior. Here the ε-constraint algorithm [3] is used to solve the MOO optimization problem. This procedure converts the multi-objective nonlinear problem (MNLP) into multiple single-objective problem (constrained nonlinear problem (CNLP)), thence minimizing only the first objective in Eq. (6), that is,

$$OF_{\varepsilon} = s\left(g^{\mathrm{E}}/RT\right) \quad (8)$$

using the other vector element to establish a constraint in the calculation, that is,

$$constraint \rightarrow s\left(h^{\mathrm{E}}\right) < \varepsilon \quad (9)$$

The value of ε is limited, from 0 to 500 J mol^{-1}, since greater errors in the h^E are not acceptable. The *efficient front* is then achieved by solving the CNLP (Eqs. (8) and (9)) for different values of ε in the indicated range. To do so, we used a hybrid evolutionary algorithm [3], coupled with Nelder-Mead algorithm [9], for local refinement.

3. Verification and selection of data series

3.1 Acetone + ethanol

There are 10 useful references in literature containing VLE data for the acetone(1) + ethanol(2) system [10–19] showing a total of 15 experimental series. In **Figure 1**, seven sets are iso-p (**Figure 1(a)**), and eight sets are iso-T (**Figure 1(b)**).

For use we refer to data series with information for the two phases. This is a requirement to check the thermodynamic consistency. **Figure 1(b)** shows an azeotrope at high pressures, which moves from the acetone-rich region toward pure ethanol as pressure increases; the separation between the compositions in the two phases is reduced. **Figure 1(c)** and **(d)** contains, respectively, the variation of γ_i and g^E/RT with the liquid composition for the system at 101 kPa. Ethanol's activity coefficient shows some errors that surely affect the global consistency of the data series. High slopes are observed as $x_1 \rightarrow 0$ along with negative values of the natural logarithm of γ_1 for data series other than those referenced [14–16]. This is a clear sign of inconsistency.

Table 1 shows the results obtained in the application of different consistency methods. The observation of the said table produces some comments which are interesting in the work development. The Wisniak test and the direct van Ness test accept most of the experimental series. The first of the methods rejects two (noted as n° 10,12) while the second fails to validate only one, n° 8. The Kojima test rejects five data series, with the error observed in the system n° 12 being critical. A new methodology recently proposed by us [6, 7] was also applied, which rejects nine systems: three by the *integral form* (n° 9, 11, 12) and six by the *differential form* (n° 1, 3, 4, 8, 9, 12). These systems present obvious signs of inconsistency that are also observed by at least one of the other methods. Therefore, the overall assessment of these series (in other words, the quality of their experimental data) is not

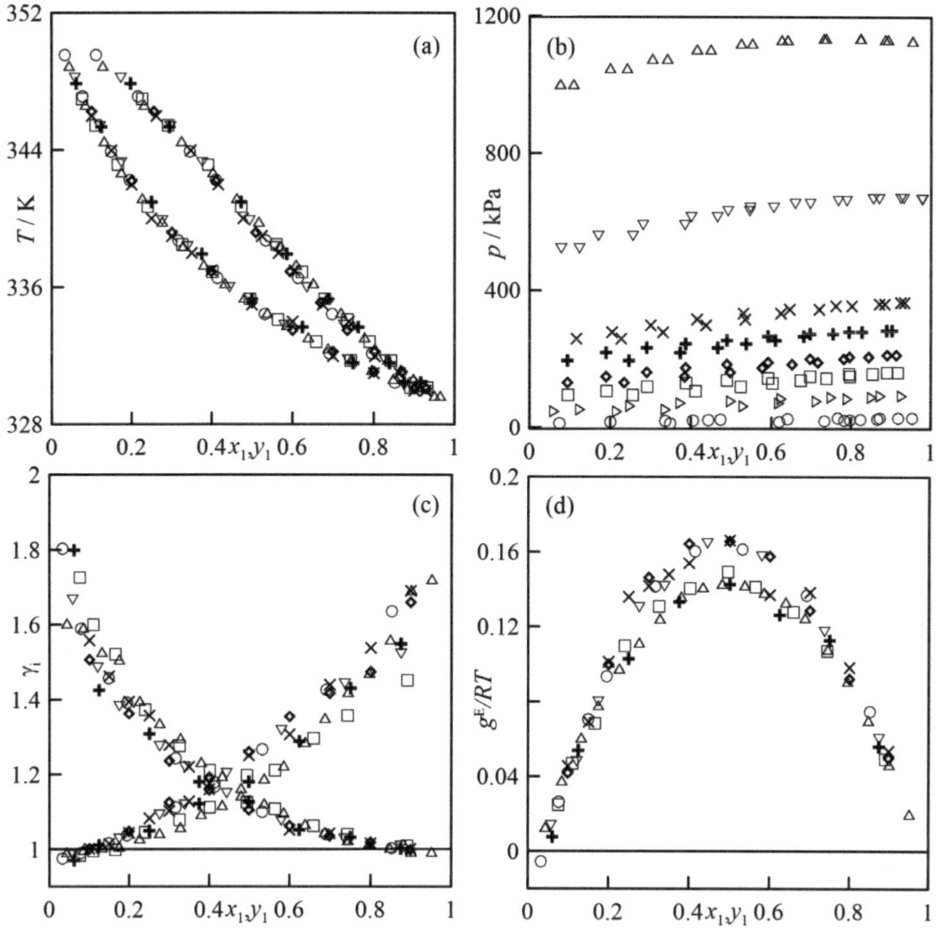

Figure 1.
Plot of VLE data of the binary: acetone(1) + ethanol(2), ***iso-p*** *≈ 101.32 kPa. (a) T,x,y; (c) γ,x; (d)* g^E/RT*,x. (×) Ref. [10]; (▽) Ref. [11]; (○) Ref. [12]; (◇) Ref. [13]; (+) Ref. [14]; (△) Ref. [15]; (□) Ref. [16]; (b) p,x,y.* ***iso-T****: (▷) Ref. [14]; (○) Ref. [17]; Ref. [18] (×) T = 372.67 K; (▽) T = 422.56 K, (△) T = 397.67 K; Ref. [19], (□) T = 344.19 K, (+) T = 363.19 K, (◇) T = 358.18 K.*

positive, ruling out the use of these series for other subsequent tasks, such as modeling and, specially, simulation.

Regarding h^E, six references were found [20–25]. All extracted values are shown in **Figure 2**(**a** and **b**), where the different series show an acceptable coherence, having $(dh^E/dT)_{p,x} > 0$.

3.2 Benzene + hexane

In studies related to the thermodynamics of solutions, the experimental information generated by the binary benzene + hexane, for different properties, has been, and still is, used by researchers in that area as a reference of their investigations; therefore, the choice of this system is justified. Twenty-three useful VLE data series were found in the bibliography [26–42], 16 iso-p and 7 iso-T. **Figure 3** shows important errors in some of the series [29, 31, 37] at 101 kPa, with data missing the trend observed in the other series. These are propagated to the T vs x,y representations (**Figure 4**(**a**)). The random error for these series is serious as evidenced in **Figure 4**(**b**).

N°	Ref.	Type	Area		Fredenslund		Wisniak		Kojima		Direct-Van Ness		Proposed test				
			d%	V	×100	V	D_w	V	$M(I_i)$	V	$\delta \ln(\gamma_1/\gamma_2)$	V	*f-int.*	V	*f-dif.*	V	VF
1	10	Iso-101 kPa	15	nv	1.9	nv	2.5	v	24	v	0.09	v	0.06	v	−0.06	nv	nv
2	11	Iso-101 kPa	13	nv	1.8	nv	2.6	v	18	v	0.09	v	0	v	0.004	v	v
3	12	Iso-101 kPa	15	nv	1.8	nv	1.7	v	10	v	0.09	v	0.14	v	−0.05	nv	nv
4	13	Iso-101 kPa	23	nv	2.2	nv	2	v	15	v	0.09	v	0.11	v	−0.08	nv	nv
5	14	Iso-101 kPa	5	nv	1.2	nv	0.5	v	27	v	0.04	v	0	v	0.003	v	v
6	15	Iso-101 kPa	7.1	nv	0.5	v	2.1	v	16	v	0.02	v	0.16	v	0.005	v	v
7	16	Iso-101 kPa	1.4	v	0.6	v	2.8	v	40	nv	0	v	0.02	v	0.006	v	v
8	14	Iso-328 K	1.7	v	0.9	v	2.1	v	74	nv	0.01	v	0.36	v	−0.050	nv	nv
9	17	Iso-298 K	41	nv	2.7	nv	1.5	v	82	nv	0.18	nv	−0.09	nv	−0.370	nv	nv
10	18	Iso-372 K	3.3	nv	0.4	v	3.3	nv	14	v	0.02	v	0.11	v	0.009	v	v
11	18	Iso-398 K	0.4	v	0.6	v	3	v	69	nv	0.02	v	−2	nv	0.001	v	nv
12	18	Iso-423 K	12	nv	0.6	v	4.4	nv	159	nv	0.01	v	−24.5	nv	−0.01	nv	nv
13	19	Iso-344 K	2.8	nv	0.3	v	2.1	v	14	v	0.01	v	0.42	v	0.016	v	v
14	19	Iso-358 K	3.3	nv	0.3	v	3	v	9	v	0.01	v	0.64	v	0.014	v	v
15	19	Iso-363 K	0.2	v	0.2	v	2.5	v	19	v	0.01	v	0.83	v	0.029	v	v

Limiting values: areas-test: $d < 2$; Fredenslund-test: $\delta y \times 100 < 1$; Wisniak-test: $D_w < 3$; Kojima-test: $M(I_i) < 30$; Direct Van Ness-test: $\delta(\ln \gamma_1/\ln \gamma_2) < 0.16$; proposed-test: f-int > 0, f-dif > 0. Header notation: V → verified; FV → fully verified. Test outcome: v → verified; nv → not verified; nd/– → not available.

Table 1.
Values obtained in the application of the thermodynamic consistency-test to VLE data of acetone + ethanol at different conditions.

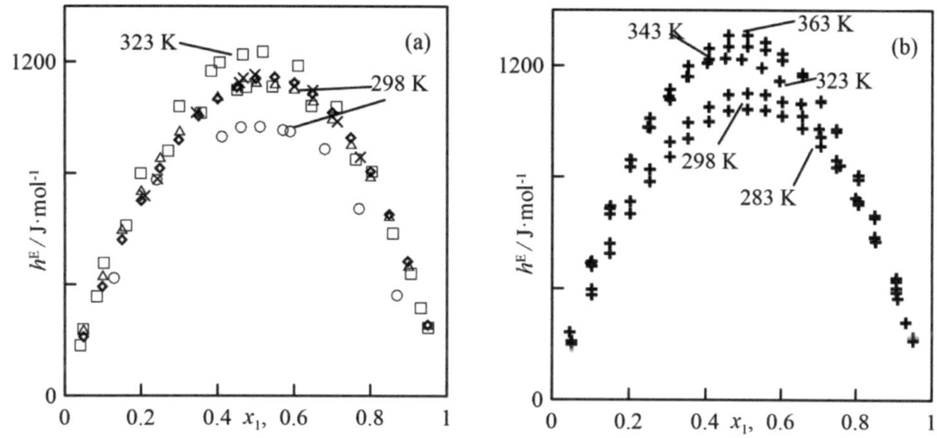

Figure 2.
h^E values for the binary acetone(1) + ethanol(2). (a) p = 101.32 kPa; (b) p = 400 kPa. (○) Ref. [20]; (×) Ref. [21]; (□) Ref. [22]; (+) Ref. [23]; (△) Ref. [24]; (◇) Ref. [25].

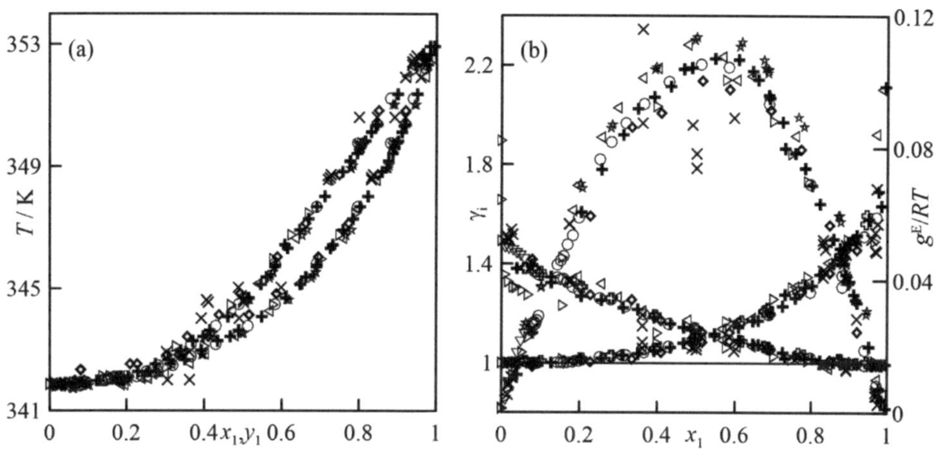

Figure 3.
Plot of iso-p VLE data of the binary benzene + hexane at 101 kPa. (a) T,x,y; (b) γ,x; g^E/RT,x. (○) Ref. [34] (✡) Ref. [35] (+) Ref. [26] (◇) Ref. [37]; (×) Ref. [29]; (▽) Ref. [32]; (▷) Ref. [31]; (◁) Ref. [37].

Figure 4 depicts the iso-*p* data set at pressures other than the atmospheric. **Figure 5(b)** indicates that three of the published series [28] (the ones that correspond to p = 610.8 kPa, 810.8 kPa, and 1013.5 kPa) show systematic errors, giving rise to $g^E/RT < 0$; thus $\gamma_i < 1$ as $x_1 \to 1$. However, the representation of T vs x,y does not reflect this anomalous behavior, so that probably they will be caused by a systematic deficiency in the monitored temperature.

Available iso-*T* data series are represented in **Figure 5**. Data are found for the whole composition interval only at 333 and 345 K. Several series were measured at 333 K [40–42], allowing their comparison. From the representation of p,x,y (**Figure 5(a)**) and related mixing quantities (**Figure 5(b)**), an acceptable coincidence is observed. Two of the data sets (Ref. [41]) show negative values of g^E/RT in the extreme points, at infinite dilution, which is a clear sign of inconsistency.

Conclusions drawn from the visual inspection are confirmed by the consistency analysis presented in **Table 2**. Data series n° 11 is discarded since consistency cannot be evaluated due to the lack of data in the zone corresponding to $x_1 > 0.2$. All consistency tests, except the direct van Ness, did not accept the series measured at

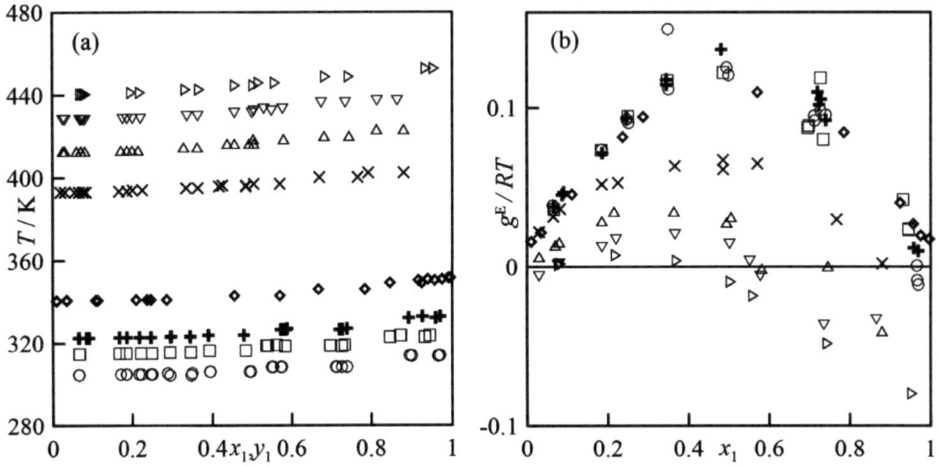

Figure 4.
Plot of iso-p VLE of the binary benzene(1) + hexane(2). (a) T,x,y; (b) g^E/RT,x. Ref. [33]: (○) p = 26 kPa; (□) p = 40 kPa; (+) p = 53 kPa; (◇) Ref. [26]; Ref. [28]: (×) p = 405.4 kPa; (△) p = 610.8 kPa; (▽) p = 810.8 kPa; (▷) p = 1013.5 kPa.

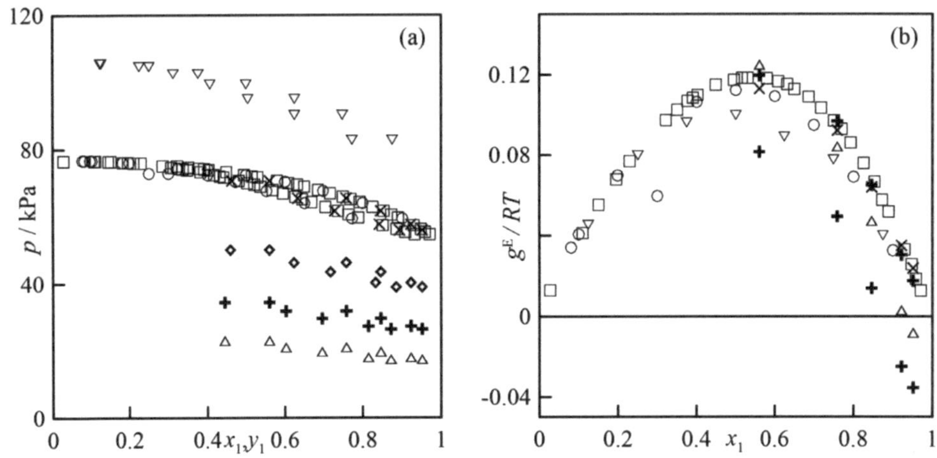

Figure 5.
Plot of iso-T VLE data of the binary benzene(1) + hexane(2). (a) p,x,y; (b) g^E/RT,x. (○) Ref. [40]; (□) Ref. [42] Ref. [41]: (+) T = 314 K; (◇) T = 323 K; (×) T = 333 K; (△) T = 303 K; (▽) Ref. [39].

the highest pressures (n° 13–16). This is due to the wrong relationship between the pure component saturation temperature (Appendix **Table A1**) and equilibrium temperature. However, it is interesting to recognize that when using other vapor pressure parameters this defect can be solved. The data series (n° 3, 4, 6–9, 19, 21–23) accepted by the proposed test [7] offer the highest consensus among all the battery of test about the quality of data, so these series could be used for subsequent tasks.

A total of 17 references were found in literature [36, 43–58] of h^E measured in the range of [293–323] K and atmospheric pressure, except those data of Yi et al. [58], at 80 kPa. **Figure 6(a)** presents the data series considered in this study. It refers to a solution with endothermic effects ($h^E \approx 900$ J mol^{-1} at $x = 0.5$ and $T = 298$ K), decreasing as temperature increases; however, the high observed dispersion of experimental values is not sufficient evidence to ensure this effect. Inspection of the h^E does not recommend excluding any of these data series; thus they will be considered in the data treatment.

N°	Ref.	Type	Area		Fredenslund		Wisniak		Kojima		Direct-Van Ness		Proposed test				
			d%	V	×100	V	D_w	V	$M(I_i)$	V	$\delta\ln(\gamma_1/\gamma_2)$	V	*f-int.*	V	*f-dif.*	V	FV
1	33	Iso-26 kPa	23.2	nv	1.2	nv	1.45	v	74	nv	0.123	v	−0.06	nv	−0.073	nv	nv
2	33	Iso-40 kPa	16.3	nv	1.2	nv	1.02	v	19	v	0.068	v	−0.02	nv	−0.013	nv	nv
3	33	Iso-53 kPa	17.5	nv	0.8	v	1.93	v	31	nv	0.063	v	0.04	v	0.001	v	v
4	26	Iso-97 kPa	19.2	nv	0.6	v	1.7	v	54	nv	0.02	v	0.05	v	0.005	v	v
5	31	Iso-101 kPa	36.5	nv	0.6	v	1.65	v	10	v	0.012	v	0.02	v	−0.047	nv	nv
6	26	Iso-101 kPa	3.6	nv	0.4	v	1.6	v	24	v	0.020	v	0.11	v	0.006	v	v
7	34	Iso-101 kPa	2.5	nv	0.3	v	1.63	v	24	v	0.004	v	0.04	v	0.007	v	v
8	35	Iso-101 kPa	1.5	v	0.1	v	1.7	v	27	v	0.003	v	0.01	v	0.014	v	v
9	37	iso-101 kPa	9	nv	0.4	v	1.75	v	44	nv	0.159	v	0.05	v	0.004	v	v
10	29	iso-101 kPa	12.3	nv	0.6	v	1.66	v	22	v	0.048	v	−0.01	nv	−0.013	nv	nv
11	32	Iso-101 kPa	nd	—	nd	—	nd	—	nd	—	nd	—	nd	—	nd	—	nv
12	37	Iso-101 kPa	9	nv	0.7	v	2.77	v	52	nv	0.043	v	0.02	v	−0.018	nv	nv
13	28	Iso-405 kPa	59	nv	1.2	nv	5.9	nv	1319	nv	0.2	nv	−0.21	nv	−0.145	nv	nv
14	28	Iso-610 kPa	58.9	nv	1.1	nv	7.51	nv	343	nv	0.043	v	−0.14	nv	−0.079	nv	nv
15	28	Iso-810 kPa	96.3	nv	2	nv	11.5	nv	291	nv	0.124	v	−0.16	nv	−0.08	nv	nv
16	28	Iso-1010 kPa	95.4	nv	3	nv	14.97	nv	6776	nv	0.364	nv	−0.07	nv	−0.192	nv	nv
17	41	Iso-303 K	16.8	nv	1.6	nv	0.61	v	670	nv	0.167	nv	0.03	v	−0.096	nv	nv
18	41	Iso-314 K	17.5	nv	2.7	nv	0.68	v	1149	nv	0.312	nv	0	nv	−0.122	nv	nv
19	41	Iso-323 K	7.9	nv	0.6	v	0.97	v	270	nv	0.048	v	0.13	v	0.006	v	v
20	40	Iso-333 K	31.1	nv	1.8	nv	2.42	v	41	nv	0.082	v	−0.33	nv	−0.048	nv	nv

N°	Ref.	Type	Area		Fredenslund		Wisniak		Kojima		Direct-Van Ness		Proposed test				
			d%	V	×100	V	D_w	V	$M(I_i)$	V	$\delta\ln(\gamma_1/\gamma_2)$	V	*f-int.*	V	*f-dif.*	V	FV
21	42	Iso-333 K	1.7	v	0.1	v	1.31	v	12	v	0.002	v	0.5	v	0.017	v	v
22	41	Iso-333 K	1.2	v	0.4	v	1.22	v	88	nv	0.017	v	0.41	v	0.009	v	v
23	39	Iso-343 K	7.4	nv	0.5	v	1.53	v	19	v	0.027	v	0.29	v	0.001	v	v

Limiting values: areas-test: $d < 2$; Fredenslund-test: $\delta y \times 100 < 1$; Wisniak-test: $D_w < 3$; Kojima-test: $M(I_i) < 30$; direct Van Ness-test: $\delta(\ln \gamma_1/\ln \gamma_2) < 0.16$; proposed-test: $f\text{-}int > 0$, $f\text{-}dif > 0$. Header notation: V → verified; FV → fully verified. Test outcome: v → verified; nv → not verified; nd/– → not available.

Table 2.
Values obtained in the application of the thermodynamic consistency-test to VLE data of benzene + hexane at different conditions.

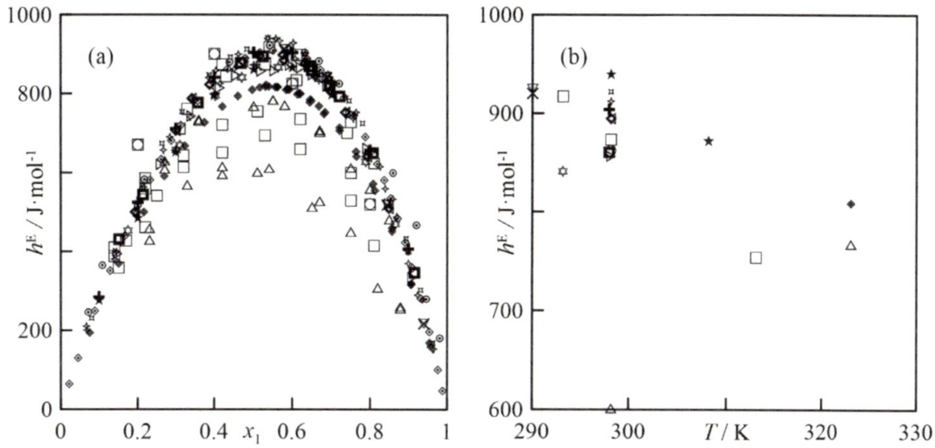

Figure 6.
Plot of h^E values for the binary benzene + hexane. (a) h^E vs x, (b) h^E (at x = 0.5) vs T. (○) Ref. [43], (□) Ref. [44], (+) Ref. [45], (◊) Ref. [46], (×) Ref. [47], (△) Ref. [48], (▽) Ref. [36], (▷) Ref. [49], (◁) Ref. [50], (□) Ref. [51], (■) Ref. [52], (✧) Ref. [53], (⌑) Ref. [54], (⦿) Ref. [55], (✡) Ref. [56], (◈) Ref. [57], (◈) Ref. [58].

4. Results and discussion

4.1 Modeling: *efficient front* and models

The VLE data series previously verified has been modeled according to the procedure described in Section 2. The *efficient fronts* obtained for each system are shown in **Figure 7**.

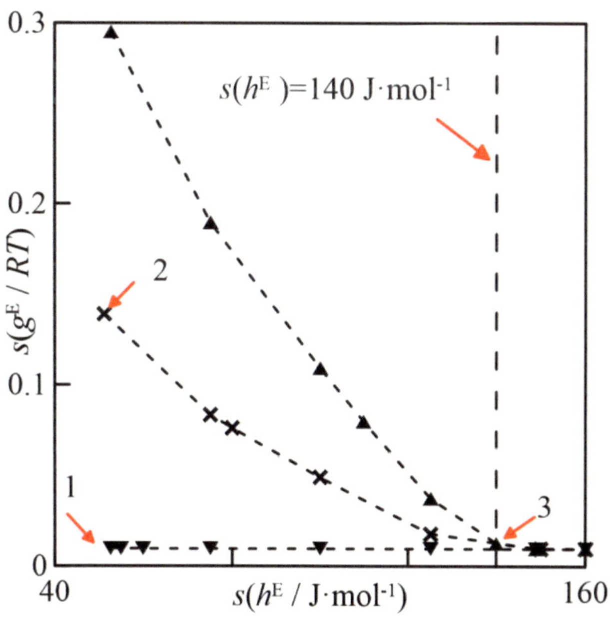

Figure 7.
Efficient fronts for $s(g^E/RT) = f(s(h^E))$, obtained for acetone + ethanol. Arrows and labels indicate the chosen results on each of the fronts, using the models: (▲) M2; (×) M3; and (▼) M4.

Acetone(1) + ethanol(2): *the efficient fronts* of results for the binary acetone + ethanol were obtained from sub-models M2, M3, and M4. Sub-model M1 did not produce an acceptable representation of the thermodynamic behavior, so it was ignored. The obtained fronts shown in **Figure 7** reveal that the three sub-models produced similar *results* when acceptable error in h^E is greater than 140 J mol^{-1}. This implies that, from this limit on, the problem becomes mono-objective, regardless of the sub-model used. For smaller errors of the h^E, $s(h^E) < 140$ J mol^{-1}, differences between sub-models M2, M3, and M4 to reproduce the VLE data are significant, reducing the maximum error by approximately $\delta s(g^E/RT) \approx 0.15$ between them. The *efficient front* achieved with model M4 shows an almost constant $s(g^E/RT)$. The other two sub-models reveal an exponential behavior as $s(h^E)$ decreases. From the set of results obtained, three of them are chosen (see **Figure 7**) to carry out a more detailed analysis on their ability to describe simultaneously the VLE and h^E. Some particular comments on those *three results* are:

- The *result* labeled as "1" (by M4) describes well the two properties under study, as seen in **Figure 8**, but at the expense of using more parameters. Specifically, this model links the state variables at equilibrium (**Figure 8(a)**), describing the observed folding at the lowest temperatures. The estimate of

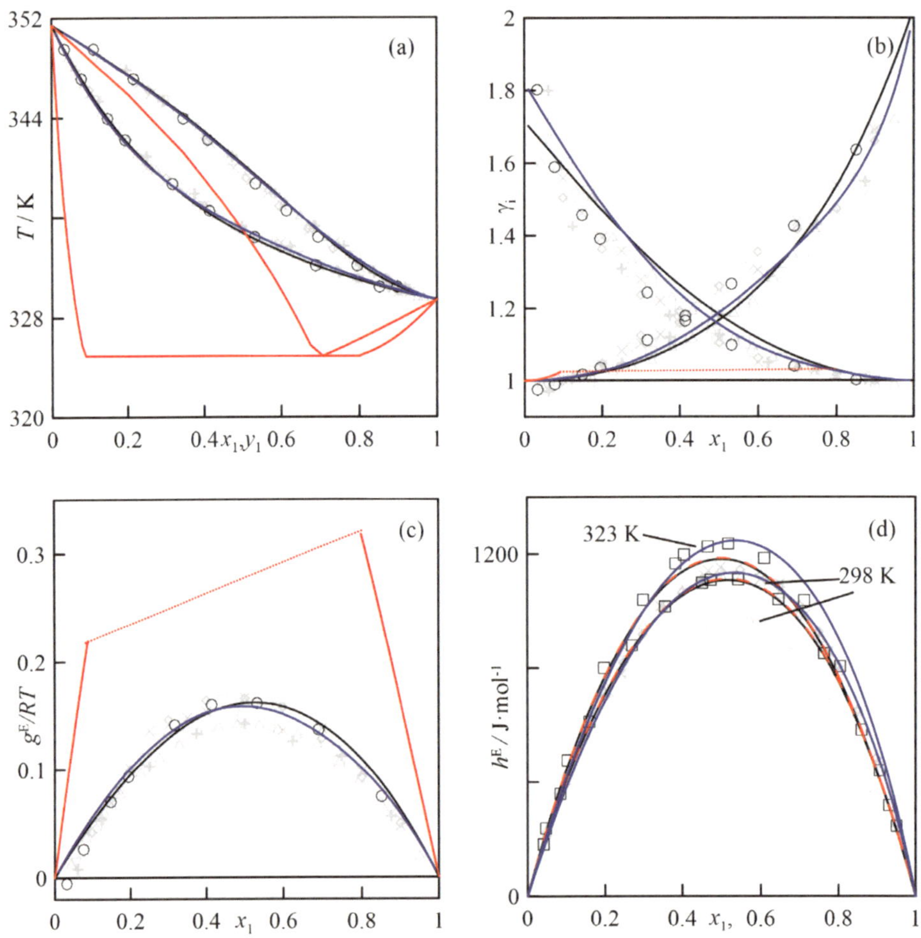

Figure 8.
*Plot of VLE at 101 kPa and h^E estimates for binary acetone(1) + ethanol(2) at 101.32 kPa. Models drawn from **Figure 7(a)**. Results (——) 1-(M4), (——) 2-(M3), (——) 3-(M3). (a) T vs x_1,y_1; (b) γ_i vs x_1; (c) g^E/RT vs x_1; (d) h^E vs x_1.*

activity coefficients (**Figure 8(b)**) is acceptable. Estimations of g^E/RT for this system are close to the set that displays the highest values. The estimate for the h^E is acceptable, although the model does not reproduce the data series extracted from Ref. [20].

- *Result* 2 (M3), which displays the highest error in the VLE estimate, wrongly estimates an azeotrope and a whole range immiscible region (**Figure 8(a)**). This poor description of the liquid phase is due to the high values of γ_i and the g^E/RT (**Figure 8(b** and **c)**). At first, the h^E is correctly represented by this parametrization, although the presence of the immiscibility truncates the validity region of the model (**Figure 8(d)**).

- *Result* 3 (M3) produces an unsatisfactory representation in the h^Es, which also presents an inversion of the thermal gradient of this property.

Final model selection should ensure that selected parametrization describes, at least qualitatively, the thermodynamic behavior closest to the real one. In this case, *result* 2 reproduces almost exactly the h^E, although it produces an incorrect g^E behavior, hence limiting its subsequent applicability. The choice between *results* 1 and 3 will depend on the influence of the h^E on the calculations in which the model is involved.

This analysis will serve as a basis to inspect the results of the remaining binary (benzene + hexane) on the results emitted by each of the models.

Benzene(1) + hexane(2): sub-model M4 was not used for the binary benzene + hexane because of the similarity with the *efficient front* produced by M3 model. Thus, sub-models M1, M2, and M3 were only applied, as shown in **Figure 9**. Sub-models M2 and M3 produce very similar results, with almost constant error, $s(g^E/RT)$, lower than 5.5×10^{-3} J mol^{-1} for all $s(h^E)$. Consequently, those *result fronts* of sub-models M1 and M2 are evaluated. The *efficient front* of sub-model M1

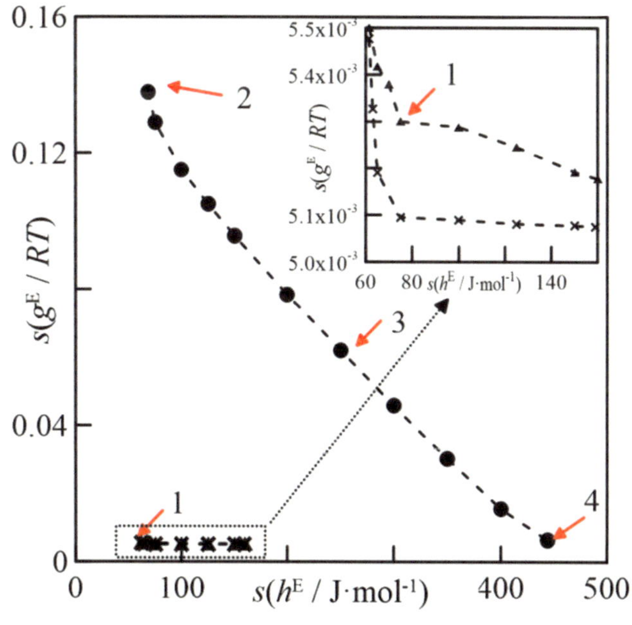

Figure 9.
Efficient fronts for $s(g^E/RT) = f(s(h^E))$, obtained for benzene + hexane. Arrows and labels indicate the chosen results on each of the fronts, using the models: (●) M1; (▲) M2; and (×) M3.

produces a quasi-linear behavior with the variation of $s(h^E)$. The difference between this *front* and that of sub-model M2 is $\delta s(g^E/RT) \approx 0.14$, when $\varepsilon = 0$. The *fronts* for models M1 and M2 do not intersect, unlike the earlier case, showing a maximum value of $s(h^E)$ at 170 J mol^{-1} and 450 J mol^{-1}, respectively. The VLE diagrams produced by the *four selected results* are shown in **Figure 10**, along with one of the validated data series for this *result.* The best description of this system is achieved with *result* 4 (M1), which reproduces the behavior of *T-x-y* experimental data (**Figure 10(a)**) and the other quantities calculated (**Figure 10(b** and **c)**). Nevertheless, the description of h^E with this model is not good. *Result* 1 (M2) produces an azeotrope at $x_1 < 0.2$, which does not occur experimentally. This poor estimation occurs even though the greater number of parameters, increasing the model's capacity to reproduce the h^E, as proven in **Figure 11**. *Results* 2 and 3 overestimate γ_i, hence g^E/RT (see **Figure 10(b** and **c)**).

This discrepancy gives rise to the formation of minimum boiling point azeotropes, which are not in accordance with experimental data. Of all the *results* chosen, only *result* 1 (belonging to sub-model M2) shows a h^E that varies significantly with temperature, since sub-model M1 is independent of this variable. The use of either *result* 2 or 3 is discouraged since their estimations of h^E, especially at temperatures other than 298 K, are not correct, in addition to the described issues in

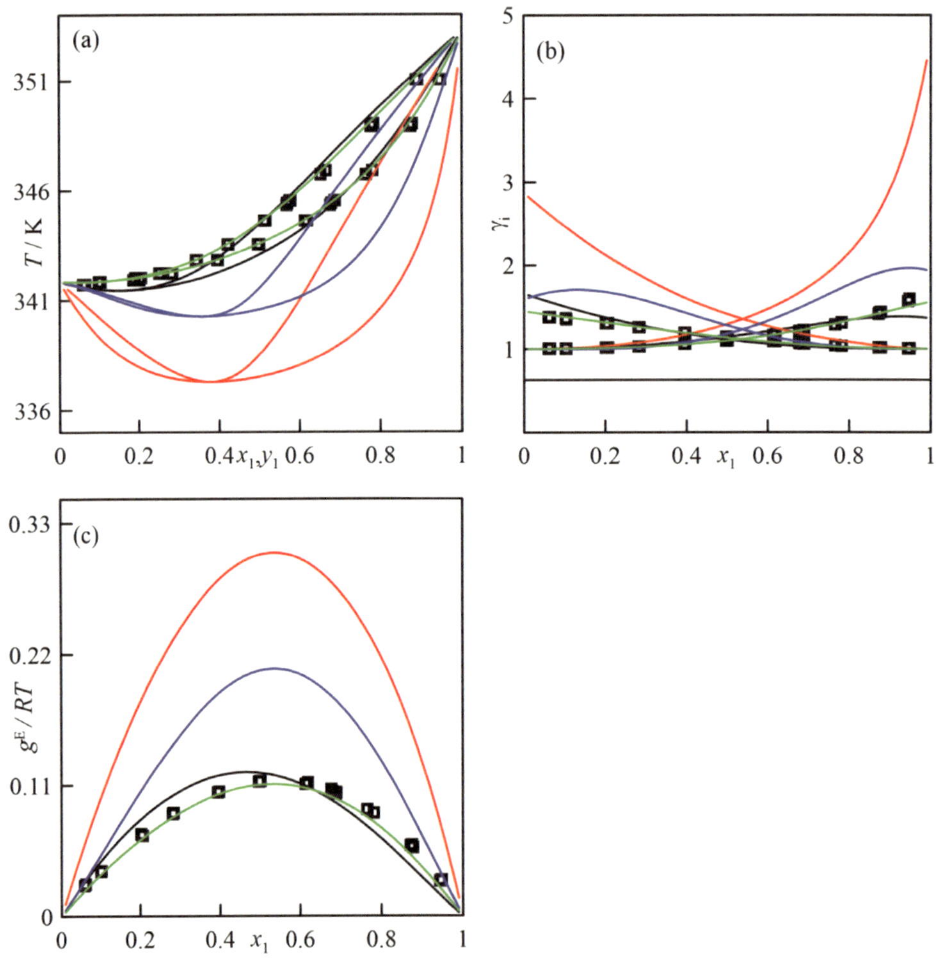

Figure 10.
Plot of VLE at 101 kPa estimates for binary benzene(1) + hexane(2). Models drawn from ***Figure 9****. Results (——) 1 (M2), (——) 2 (M1), (——) 3 (M1) and 4 (——) (M1). (a) T vs x,y; (b)γ vs x; (c)* g^E*/RT vs x.*

representing the phase equilibria. This being said, *result 3* represents the average behavior of this property in the working range.

From previous observations, *result* 4 (M1) is recommended for those cases where the h^E plays a secondary role in comparison to the reliable reproduction of the VLE diagram. Otherwise, *result* 1 (M2) is preferred, despite the qualitative misfit to experimental data. **Table 3** presents an overview of the present section with a summary of the models to be used in the simulation task.

4.2 Simulation results of a rectification process for each of the studied dissolutions

The models obtained previously are used in the design of a simulation operation comparing their capacity in terms of some operation variables such as composition and temperature profiles, as well as energy consumption. General conditions for the simulations are summarized in **Table 4**. In all cases, columns are fed with a 1 kmol/h at equimolar composition of the corresponding solution, at 298.15 K and 101.32 kPa. Simulations are performed using the RadFrac block of AspenPlus© V8.8 (AspenOne©, [59]).

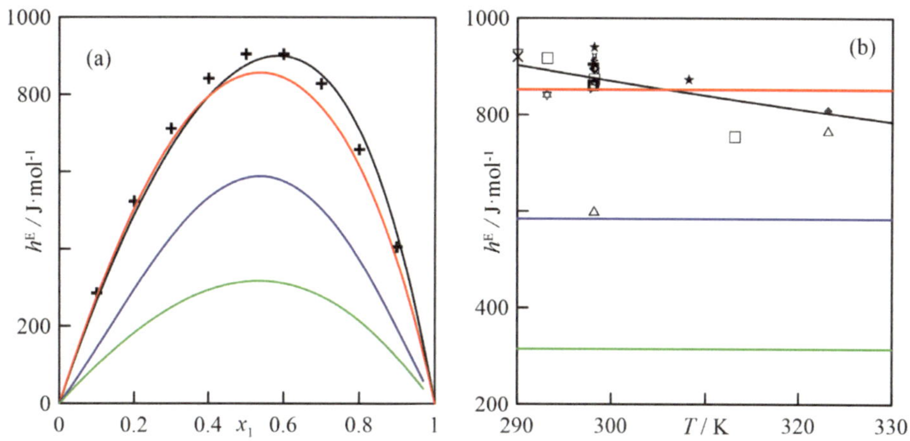

Figure 11.
*Estimation of h^E values at 101.32 kPa using the different results indicated in the fronts of **Figure 9** for benzene (1) + hexane(2). (a) h^E vs x_1 (T = 298.15 K), (b) h^E vs T (x_1 = 0.5). Results (——) 1 (M2); (——) 2 (M1); (——) 3 (M1); (——) 4 (M1).*

System	M1	M2	M3	M4
Acetone + ethanol	×	✓	✓✓	✓✓
Benzene + hexane	✓✓	✓✓	✓	×

✓✓ → *used for modeling and simulation;* ✓ → *used for modeling;* × → *not used.*

Table 3.
List of sub-models applied to each system.

Binary system	Reflux ratio	Distillate rate (kmol/h)	n° stages	Feed stage
Acetone + ethanol	6	0.5	22	16
Benzene + hexane	10	0.6	30	20

Table 4.
Operation data for the rectification columns to separate the binaries.

Acetone(1) + ethanol(2): the simulation of a rectification column to purify the acetone+ethanol binary system, using the *result* labeled as "2" in **Figure** 7, does not provide a coherent resolution because it estimates the presence of two immiscible liquid phases. The final values obtained with *results* 1 and 3 are detailed in **Table 5**, while the composition profiles are shown in **Figure 12**. In both cases the composition of the distillate is higher than 99% in acetone and at the same temperature in the stage.

The exact purity is slightly higher with *result* 1 than with *result* 3, the difference being 0.2%. The calculation in the bottoms of the tower reveals differences between the two parametrizations, giving place to an effluent somewhat purer in the case of *result* 1. The difference between both models is 0.001 in molar fraction. These observations directly affect the calculation of the energy balance and, therefore, to the consumed energy. Thus, the consumption in the condenser is estimated similarly with both parametrizations, while that of the reboiler is significantly higher with *result* 3, due to the greater quantity of ethanol and the incorrect estimate of other quantities, such as the mixing enthalpies.

Stage	*Result* 1 (M4)			*Result* 3 (M3)		
	x_1	y_1	T/K	x_1	y_1	T/K
1	0.990	0.993	329.0	0.989	0.991	329.0
5	0.974	0.981	329.1	0.970	0.978	329.1
9	0.941	0.957	329.3	0.935	0.953	329.4
13	0.853	0.900	330.1	0.846	0.894	330.2
17	0.518	0.709	334.4	0.526	0.710	334.2
22	0.010	0.031	350.6	0.011	0.035	350.5
Q_c/kJ h^{-1}		1.035E5			1.034E5	
Q_r/kJ h^{-1}		1.038E5			1.044E5	

Table 5.
Quantities obtained in the simulation of a separation process for the binary acetone(1) + ethanol(2), using different values from the efficient front *shown in* **Figure 7**.

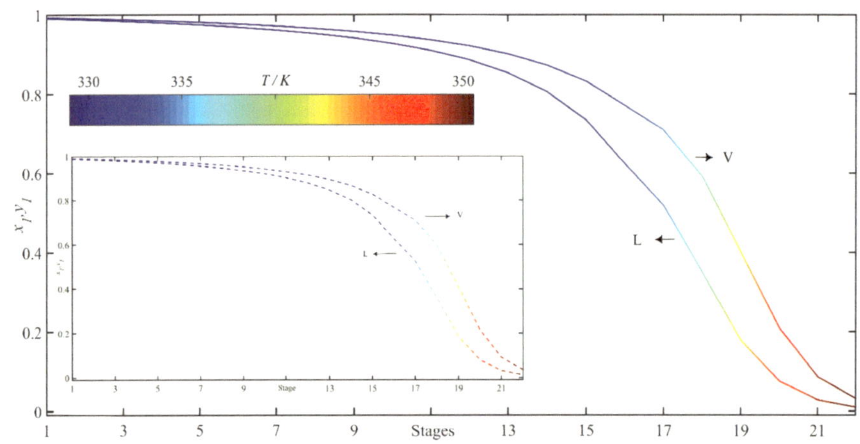

Figure 12.
Plot of composition and temperature profiles obtained in the simulation of a separation operation for acetone (1) + ethanol(2) system, using the different parametrizations proposed: (—) 1 (M4). L, liquid stream profile; V, vapor stream profile.

The composition profiles and temperature gradient of the two tested solutions present similar qualitative behaviors. Most of the column is used as an enriching region which requires a high number of stages in both cases.

Benzene(1) + hexane(2): values obtained in the simulation of the distillation operation of this binary dissolution are in **Table 6**, while composition and temperature profiles are plotted in **Figure 13**. For the first three *results* (1, 2, and 3), the presence of an azeotrope limits the distillate composition. Thus, *result* 1 produces an effluent with a benzene composition of 16.7% (v/v), while for *results* 2 and 3, the compositions are, respectively, 37.2 and 30.9%. The simulation carried out with the parametrization of *result* 4 produces a purer distillate of 15.6%, due to the absence of the azeotrope. However, the folding effect observed between the equilibrium curves in experimental data as well as the diagram estimated by *result* 4 complicates the separation beyond this point. This justifies that the composition profiles are similar to results 1 and 4 (see **Figure 13**).

The residual streams obtained by *results* 1 and 4 contain benzene with a purity higher than 99.9%, while the other two *results* do not produce the separation of the

Stage	*Result* 1 (M2)			*Result* 2 (M1)			*Result* 3 (M1)			*Result* 4 (M1)		
	x_1	y_1	T/K	x_1	y_1	T/K	x_1	y_1	T/K	x_1	y_1	T/K
1	0.167	0.161	341.3	0.372	0.372	337.3	0.310	0.309	340.1	0.167	0.156	341.7
5	0.201	0.189	341.3	0.372	0.372	337.3	0.312	0.311	340.1	0.220	0.202	341.9
10	0.280	0.250	341.6	0.372	0.372	337.3	0.319	0.316	340.1	0.310	0.278	342.2
15	0.505	0.414	343.1	0.374	0.373	337.3	0.337	0.330	340.1	0.473	0.407	343.2
20	0.842	0.740	348.5	0.405	0.388	337.4	0.392	0.369	340.2	0.772	0.663	346.8
25	0.991	0.982	352.6	0.409	0.390	337.4	0.422	0.389	340.3	0.988	0.975	352.4
30	1.000	0.999	352.8	0.692	0.510	338.8	0.785	0.631	344.0	1.000	0.999	352.8
Q_c/kJ h^{-1}	1.829E5			1.988E5			1.686E5			1.804E5		
Q_r/kJ h^{-1}	1.886E5			2.050E5			1.802E5			1.898E5		

Table 6.
Quantities obtained in the simulation of a distillation process for the binary benzene(1) + hexane(2), using different values from the efficient front *shown in **Figure 9**.*

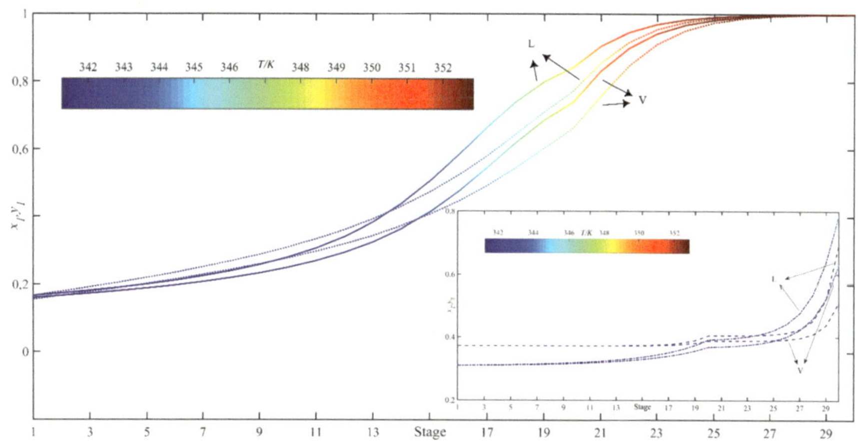

Figure 13.
Plot of composition and temperature profiles obtained in the simulation of a separation operation for the binary benzene(1) + hexane(2), using the different parametrizations proposed: (——) 1 (M2); (- - - -) 2 (M1); (……) 4 (M1). L, liquid stream profile; V, vapor stream profile.

binary dissolution with high purities (no more than 79%), due to the presence of the azeotrope at intermediate composition. The differences noted in compositions in the head and bottom of the column cause that the corresponding temperatures are also different. Between *results* 1 and 4, there is a difference in temperature of almost 0.5 K, while *results* 2 and 3 estimate lower temperatures by more than 1 K with respect to the others. In this case, the modeling errors in another of properties, such as excess enthalpies, as well as the differences in the output composition, also affects to produce noteworthy differences in the energetic consumptions of both condenser and boiler. In this sense, similar results are obtained for *results* 1 and 4, although, a priori, it is not possible to indicate which of these is closer to the true behavior of the column.

5. Conclusions

The aim of this work is to present the practice carried out on a set of operations constituting a procedure involving the following sequences: experimentation ↔ verification ↔ modeling ↔ simulation. A description of the last three operations is proposed since the necessary experimental information (iso-p and iso-T VLE data and h^E) was extracted from the available publications. The proposed methodology is applied to two significant binary systems in the dissolution thermodynamic field, such as acetone-ethanol and benzene-hexane. The data checking is carried out with different classical methods, which is recommended in the recent literature [6]. In addition, a rigorous method recently designed by the authors [7] was also used in order to guarantee the quality of the experimental data used. This method has the advantage of offering some information about the origin of deficiencies in the experimental data.

A polynomial expression was used in the *modeling* step (see Eqs. (1) and (3)), used in the correlation of thermodynamic properties, from which four sub-models (M1–M4) are established in Section 2.1, depending on the availability of data for each system to avoid overfitting. Modeling in all cases was performed on the Gibbs dimensionless function, g^E/RT (VLE), and on h^E data, two-objective optimization approach addressed as a sequence of mono-objective subproblems according to the ε-constraint algorithm. A set of models are selected from the attained *efficient fronts* to provide a rationale on the trade-off decision task that is supposed to yield the final model for later uses, such as design/simulation. For the two studied cases, these *fronts* reveal a quasi-linear trend (with a negative slope) when the number of parameters used in the model is small. *Efficient fronts'* slope decreases as the number of parameters increases, until the error of VLE delinks to that of the h^E for highly flexible models.

The rectification of the selected systems was simulated using the *RadFrac* block of AspenPlus© with the selected thermodynamic parametrizations. For the binary acetone + ethanol, some models showed an immiscible region, not reflected by the experimental information, giving rise to incoherent simulations. Two models gave rise to inexistent azeotropes in the benzene + hexane dissolution, with incorrect results in the simulation. On the other hand, errors in the excess enthalpy estimates did not influence on the procedure simulation, but it should be noted that it has an important role in the modeling of binary systems. In summary, the influence of a certain set of parameters on the simulation varies depending on each particular system. Besides, it is observed that, as the number of parameters grows in a model, the optimization problem mutes toward a mono-objective one since the considered criteria are invariant in one another. In these cases, taking the set of parameters that present the lowest error on h^E is the best option. However, increasing the number of parameters might lead to overfitting if not enough attention is paid to the model extrapolation capabilities.

Acknowledgements

This work was supported by the Ministerio de Economía y Competitividad (MINECO) of the Spanish Government, Grant CTQ2015-68428-P. One of us (AS) is also grateful to the ACIISI (from Canaries Government, No. 2015010110) for the support received. This work is a result of the Project "AIProcMat@N2020—Advanced Industrial Processes and Materials for a Sustainable Northern Region of Portugal 2020," with the reference NORTE-01-0145-FEDER-000006, supported by Norte Portugal Regional Operational Programme (NORTE 2020), under the Portugal 2020 Partnership Agreement, through the European Regional Development Fund (ERDF); Associate Laboratory LSRE-LCM—UID/EQU/50020/2019—funded by national funds through FCT/MCTES (PIDDAC).

A. Vapor pressure modeling

Vapor pressures of pure compounds are calculated using Antoine equation:

$$\log p_i^o / kPa = A - B / [T/K - C] \tag{10}$$

Parameters A, B, and C, from literature [60–62], are shown in **Table A1**.

	A	*B*	C	Ref.
Acetone	6.42448	1312.25	32.45	[60]
Ethanol	7.24677	1598.67	46.42	[61]
Benzene	6.03053	1211.03	52.36	[62]
Hexane	5.87891	1089.49	60.55	[62]

Table A1.
Parameters of Antoine equation for pure compounds in this work.

Author details

Adriel Sosa[1], Luís Fernández[1], Elena Gómez[2], Eugénia A. Macedo[2] and Juan Ortega[2]*

1 Grupo de Ingeniería Térmica e Instrumentación (IDeTIC), Parque Científico-Tecnológico, Universidad de Las Palmas de Gran Canaria, Canary Islands, Spain

2 Associate Laboratory of Separation and Reaction Engineering and Laboratory of Catalysis and Materials (LSRE-LCM), Department of Chemical Engineering, Faculty of Engineering, University of Porto, Porto, Portugal

*Address all correspondence to: juan.ortega@ulpgc.es

References

[1] Luyben WL. Process Modeling, Simulation and Control for Chemical Engineers. 2nd ed. NewYork: McGraw-Hill; 1989

[2] Turton R, Baille RC, Whiting WB, Shaelwitz JA. Analysis, Synthesis, and Design of Chemical Processes. 3th ed. Boston: Prentice Hall; 1998

[3] Coello C, Lamont G, Van Veldhuisen D. Evolutionary Algorithms for Solving Multi-objective Problems. 2nd ed. Berlin: Springer; 2007

[4] Nocedal J, Wright SJ. Numerical Optimization. 2nd ed. Berlin: Springer; 2006

[5] Deb K. Multi-Objective Optimization Using Evolutionary Algorithms. New Jersey: Wiley; 2001

[6] Wisniak J, Ortega J, Fernández L. A fresh look at the thermodynamic consistency of vapor-liquid equilibria data. The Journal of Chemical Thermodynamics. 2016;**105**:355-365

[7] Fernández L, Ortega J, Wisniak J. A rigorous method to evaluate the consistency of experimental data in phase equilibria. Application to VLE and VLLE. AICHE Journal. 2017;**63**: 5125-5148

[8] Ortega J, Espiau F, Wisniak J. New parametric model to correlate the excess Gibbs function and thermodynamic properties of multicomponent systems. Application to binary systems. Industrial and Engineering Chemistry Research. 2010;**49**:406-421

[9] Lagarias JC, Reeds JA, Wright MH, Wright PE. Convergence properties of the Nelder-Mead simplex method in low dimensions. SIAM Journal on Optimization. 1998;**9**:112-147

[10] Chu JC, Getty RJ, Brennecke JF, Paul R. Distillation Equilibrium Data. New York: Reinhold; 1950

[11] Hellwig LR, Van Winkle M. Vapour-liquid equilibria for ethyl alcohol binary systems. Industrial and Engineering Chemistry. 1953;**45**:624-629

[12] Amer HH, Paxton RR, Van Winkle M. Methanol-ethanol-acetone vapor-liquid equilibria. Industrial and Engineering Chemistry. 1956;**48**: 142-146

[13] Morachevskii AG, Leontév NP. Liquid vapor equilibrium in the ternary system acetone chloroform ethyl alcohol. Zhurnal Fizicheskoi Khimii. 1960;**34**:2347-2349

[14] Vinichenko IG, Susarev MP. Study and calculation of the liquid-vapor equilibrium in the acetone-ethanol-hexane system. Zhurnal Pikladnoi Khimii. 1966;**39**:1583-1587

[15] Ku H-C, Tu C-H. Isobaric vapor liquid equilibria for mixtures of acetone, ethanol, and 2,2,4-trimethylpentane at 101.3 kPa. Fluid Phase Equilibria. 2005; **231**:99-108

[16] Chen S, Bao Z, Lu Z, Yang Y, Xu W, Chen Z, et al. Vapor liquid equilibrium for the 1,1,1-trifluorotrichloroethane + sulfuryl chloride system at 101.3 kPa. Journal of Chemical & Engineering Data. 2014;**59**:16-21

[17] Kato M. Analysis of the excess Gibbs energies of binary mixtures using non-randomness factors determined from excess volume data. Bulletin of the Chemical Society of Japan. 1982;**55**:23-27

[18] Campbell SW, Wilsak RA, Thodos G. Vapor-liquid equilibrium measurements for the ethanol-acetone

system at 327.7, 397.7, and 422.6 K. Journal of Chemical & Engineering Data. 1987;**32**:357-362

[19] Lee MJ, Hu C-H. Isothermal vapor-liquid equilibria for mixtures of ethanol, acetone, and diisopropyl ether. Fluid Phase Equilibria. 1995;**109**:83-98

[20] Paz-Andrade MI, Jimenez E, Lopez-Garcia D. Excess enthalpies for the systems acetone + ethanol, acetone + 1-pentanol and acetone + 1-hexanol at 25 c. Anales de Quimica. 1973;**69**:289-294

[21] Coomber BA, Wormald CJ. A stirred flow calorimeter: The excess enthalpies of acetone+water and of acetone+some normal alcohols. The Journal of Chemical Thermodynamics. 1976;**8**:793-799

[22] Nicolaides GL, Eckert CA. Experimental heats of mixing of some miscible and partially miscible nonelectrolyte systems. Journal of Chemical & Engineering Data. 1978;**23**:152-156

[23] Lietzmann A, Loewen B, Schulz S. Excess molar enthalpies of propanone + heptane, propanone + ethanol, ethanol + heptane, and 2-propanol + water at 283.15, 298.15, 323.15, 343.15, and 363.15 K. Journal of Chemical & Engineering Data. 1994;**39**:785-788

[24] Nagata I, Ksiazczak A. Excess enthalpies for (ethanol + propanone) and (ethanol + propanone + benzene) at the temperature 298.15 K. The Journal of Chemical Thermodynamics. 1994;**26**:165-169

[25] Lien P-J, Lin HM, Lee MJ. Excess molar enthalpies for binary mixtures of ethanol + acetone, +octane, +cyclohexane and 1-propanol + acetone, +octane, +heptane at 323.15 K. Journal of Chemical & Engineering Data. 2003;**48**:359-361

[26] Tongberg CO, Johnston F. Vapor-liquid equilibria for n-hexane-benzene mixtures. Industrial and Engineering Chemistry. 1933;**25**:733-735

[27] Myers HS. Vapor-liquid equilibrium data for binary mixtures of paraffins and aromatics. Industrial and Engineering Chemistry. 1955;**47**:2215-2219

[28] Kumarkrishna Rao VN, Swami DR, Narasinga Rao N. Vapor-liquid equilibriums of benzene-hexane and benzene-cyclohexane systems systems. AICHE Journal. 1957;**3**:191-197

[29] Gothard F, Minea I. Revista De Chimie. 1960;**11**:642

[30] Gothard F, Minea I, Grigoras C. Revista De Chimie. 1960;**11**:705

[31] Brzostowski W. Vapour-liquid equilibria in the benzene + hexane system containing carbon 1 4-labelled benzene. Bull. Acad. Pol. Sci.-Chim. 1961;**9**:471-475

[32] Gotthard F, Minea I. Rectification of n-hexane + benzene mixtures and the liquid-vapor equilibrium of these mixtures. Revista De Chimie. 1961;**12**:489-493

[33] Gothard F, Minea I. Vapor-liquid equilibrium of hexane+benzene mixtures at low pressures. Revista De Chimie. 1963;**14**:520-525

[34] Butler PA, Ridgway K. Ternary vapour-liquid equilibrium: The use of a multi-stage still. Journal of Applied Chemistry. 1967;**17**:191-197

[35] Hanson DO, Van Winkle M. Alteration of the relative volatility of n-hexane-1-hexene by oxygenated and chlorinated solvents. Journal of Chemical & Engineering Data. 1967;**12**:319

[36] Ridgway K, Butler PA. Some physical properties of the ternary system benzene-cyclohexane-n-hexane. Journal of Chemical & Engineering Data. 1967;**12**:509-515

[37] Michishita T, Arai Y, Saito S. Vapor-liquid equilibria of hydrocarbons at atmospheric pressure. Kagaku Kogaku. 1971;**35**:111-116

[38] Barhala A, Gothard FA, Marchidan DI. Liquid-vapor equilibria in binary mixtures of 2-chlorotoluene + 4-chlorotoluene and toluene + 2-chlorotoluene. Revue Roumaine de Chimie. 1992;**37**:27-40

[39] Susarev MP, Chen S-T. Calculation of liquid-vapor equilibrium for ternary systems from data on binary systems-the system benzene-n-hexane-cyclohexane. Zhurnal Fizicheskoi Khimii. 1963;**37**:1739-1744

[40] Beyer W, Schuberth H, Leibnitz E. Journal für Praktische Chemie. 1965;**27**:276

[41] Li IPC, Wong YW, Chang S-D, Lu BC-Y. Vapor-liquid equilibriums in systems n-hexane-benzene and n-pentane-toluene. Journal of Chemical & Engineering Data. 1972;**17**:492-498

[42] Saez C, Compostizo A, Rubio RG, Crespo-Colin A, Diaz Pena M. *p, T, x, y*, data of benzene + n-hexane and cyclohexane + n-heptane systems. Fluid Phase Equilibria. 1985;**24**:241-258

[43] Baud E. Thermodynamic analysis of binary mixtures. Bulletin de la Société Chimique de France. 1915;**17**:329-345

[44] Kireev VA. Heats of mixing of liquids. 3. Integral and partial heats of mixing of normal liquids. Acta Physicochimica URSS. 1937;7:363-373

[45] Kuhn W, Massini P. Heat of mixing and azeotrope formation in non-polar liquids. Helvetica Chimica Acta. 1950;**33**:737-765

[46] Mathieson AR, Thynne JCJ. Thermodynamics of hydrocarbon mixtures. II. The heats of mixing of the binary mixtures formed by benzene, cyclohexane, heptane, toluene, and hexane. Journal of the Chemical Society. 1956:3708-3713

[47] Schnaible HW, Van Ness HC, Smith JM. Heats of mixing of liquids. AICHE Journal. 1957;**3**:147-152

[48] Jones HKD, Lu BC-Y. Heats of mixing of liquids for the system ethanol-benzene-n-hexane. Journal of Chemical & Engineering Data. 1966;**11**:488-492

[49] Paz Andrade MI, Regueiro M, Baluja MC, Jimenez Cuesta E, Hernandez C. Heats of mixing at mean temperatures hexane+benzene system. Acta Científica Compostelana. 1970;**7**:147-154

[50] Paz Andrade MI. International DATA Series, Selected Data on Mixtures, Series A. 1973;**2**:97-104

[51] Diaz Pena M, Menduina C. Excess enthalpies at 323.15 K of binary mixtures of benzene with n-alkanes. The Journal of Chemical Thermodynamics. 1974;**6**:1097-1102

[52] Romani L, Paz Andrade MI. Thermodynamic excess functions at 25 C. III. benzene+hexane isomers. Anales de Quimica. 1974;**70**:422-425

[53] Christensen C, Gmehling J, Rasmussen P, Weidlich U. Heats of mixture data collection. In: DECHEMA Chemistry Data Series. Vol. III. Frankfurt/Main; 1984

[54] Bao J, Xie Y, Zhang K, Hu Y. A study on the excess enthalpies for the ternary system benzene-cyclohexane-n-hexane. Huadong Huagong Xueyuan Xuebao. 1985;**11**:467-478

[55] Hwang C-A, Elkabule AS, Whitman DL, Miller RC. Excess molar enthalpies of (benzene + cyclohexane + n-hexane).

The Journal of Chemical Thermodynamics. 1987;**19**:1031-1036

[56] Casado H, Segade L, Franjo C, Jimenez E, Paz Andrade MI. Excess molar enthalpies of propyl propanoate + hexane + benzene at 298.15 and 308.15 K. Journal of Chemical & Engineering Data. 2000;**45**:445-449

[57] Mato MM, Balseiro J, Jimenez E, Legido JL, Galinanes AV, Paz-Andrade MI. Excess molar enthalpies and excess molar volumes of the ternary system 1,2-dichlorobenzene+benzene+hexane at 298.15 K. Journal of Chemical & Engineering Data. 2002;**47**:1436-1441

[58] Yi CK, Park Y, You S-S. Measurement of excess enthalpies using a high-pressure flow microcalorimeter and determination of binary interaction parameters for thermodynamic models. Korean Journal of Chemical Engineering. 2009;**26**:220-224

[59] Aspen Technologies Inc. Aspen Physical Properties System. UK: Cambridge; 2004

[60] Ambrose D, Sprake CHS, Townsend R. Thermodynamic properties of organic oxygen compounds XXXIII. The vapour pressure of acetone. The Journal of Chemical Thermodynamics. 1974;**6**: 693-700

[61] Ambrose D, Sprake CHS. Thermodynamic properties of organic oxygen compounds XXV. Vapour pressures and normal boiling temperatures of aliphatic alcohols. The Journal of Chemical Thermodynamics. 1970;**2**:631-645

[62] Riddick JA, Bunger WB, Sakano TK. Organic solvents: Physical properties and methods of purification. In: Techniques of Chemistry. 4th ed. Vol. II. New York: Wiley-Interscience; 1986

Chapter 5

Azeotrope-Breaking Potential of Binary Mixtures in Phase Equilibria Modeling

Sergey Artemenko and Victor Mazur

Abstract

Global phase diagrams (GPD) of binary mixtures in phase equilibria modeling are analyzed. The mapping of the global equilibrium surface in the parameter space of the equation of state (EoS) model provides the most comprehensive system of criteria for predicting binary mixture phase behavior. One may obtain the relationships for azeotropic boundaries from the global phase diagram [*A* (azeotrope) and *H* (hetero-azeotrope)] regions. Analytical expressions to predict *azeotrope* and *double azeotrope* phenomena in terms of critical parameters of pure components were derived using global phase diagram. The problem estimations of phase behavior modeling under the uncertainty are formulated applying the Pareto-optimum parameter and different (crisp and fuzzy) convolution schemes. The Pareto-optimum parameters in the Redlich-Kwong equation of state used different conflicting data sets (simultaneous description of the phase equilibria and critical line data in binary mixtures, thermodynamically consistent description of the inhomogeneous data). Ionic liquids (ILs) are one of prospective new working media for different environmentally friendly technologies. Practically undetectable vapor pressure is considered the ILs as ideal solvents replacing conventional solvents in the frame of a "green chemistry." Combination of ionic liquids with conventional natural and synthetic refrigerants promotes the increasing efficiency of absorption processes due to nonvolatile ionic liquids (absorbents).

Keywords: azeotrope, phase equilibria, global phase diagram, equation of state, the Pareto-optimum parameters, azeotrope-breaking, ionic liquids, refrigerant blends

1. Introduction

The pioneering work of Van Konynenburg and Scott [1] demonstrated that the van der Waals one-fluid model has wide possibilities of qualitative reproducing the main types of phase diagrams of binary mixtures. The thermodynamic equilibrium mapping onto the space of parameters of an equation of state gives the possibility to obtain the criteria for the phase behavior of binary mixtures. The functions of temperature T, pressure p, chemical potential μ, and component concentration x are determined as the "field" variables that are the same for all phases coexisting in equilibrium of a substance i. The molar fraction is the "density" that is in principle of liquid *(l)* and gas *(g)* phases. Global phase diagrams (GPD) of binary mixtures

IntechOpen

represent boundaries between types of phase behavior in a dimensionless space of EOS parameters.

GPD also provides good visualization of the impact of model parameters of mixture components to the topology of phase behavior. The proposed types of phase behavior classification [1] are generally used to characterize the different types of phase behavior in binary mixtures.

Varchenko [2] has provided a more rigorous classification for conventional features of equilibrium surface and phase diagrams for binary mixtures with strict determination of the eight topologically different rearrangements.

Current topological analysis of equilibrium surfaces of binary fluid systems provides 26 singularities and 56 scenarios of phase behavior evolution depicted in p–T diagrams [3].

The various phase diagram classes and p–T projections of the main types of phase diagrams have been described in literature [1–3]. Global phase diagrams are a technique which can be used for the prediction of different phase behavior in the mixtures without vapor–liquid equilibrium calculations [4–11].

Patel and Sunol [12] developed a robust automated routine for global phase diagram generation in binary systems. The approach uses any equation of state models, takes into account solid-phase existence, and provides type VI phase diagram generation. The generated data set includes calculations of the critical endpoints, quadruple points, critical azeotrope points, azeotrope endpoints, pure azeotrope points, critical line, liquid–liquid–vapor line, and azeotrope line.

Azeotrope-breaking is important for the successful distilling of industrially important mixtures. To simulate the mixture phase behavior, models based on the equation of state (EoS) presentation for thermodynamic properties are more preferable. The conventional methods of parameter identification use the statistical paradigm, which is based on maximum likelihood or a posteriori probability criteria and does not take into account uncertainties of vague nature. Decision-making process under various uncertainties requires mathematical methods, which include uncertainty evaluation a priori. Statistical methods interpret all variety of uncertainty types in the framework of the randomness concept. Nevertheless, there are ill-structured situations, which have not any strictly defined boundaries and cannot be accurately formulated.

The main challenge is to deal with such kind of expressions like "neighborhood" or "best fit," which do not have strict boundaries, separating one class of objects from others. Generally, there are ambiguous verbal models, which can be treated as fuzzy formulated targets, depending on biased assessment of boundaries for approximations used. As a case study, we provide estimation of the optimal parameters of the Redlich-Kwong equation of state [13], retrieved from the different conflicting data sets resulting from the inconsistency problems arising in the modeling of phase equilibria. Such process reflects different types of uncertainties, including uncertainties of nonstatistical origin. The parameters of phase equilibria models are considered as alternatives, i.e., they allow meeting the targets and prescribed constraints. The parameter estimation problem of phase equilibrium modeling multicriteria approach is applied. To describe the uncertainties of such type, the "fuzzy set" approach introduced by L.A. Zadeh [14] is used.

The problem of optimum parameter estimation of thermodynamic and phase behavior under the uncertainty is a search of the Pareto set. The diverse computational methods of the Pareto-optimum parameter convolution crisp and fuzzy schemes to reduce a vector criterion into the scalar are provided.

Ionic liquids can be treated as "adjustable" working fluids given the fact that variations of different "R – " groups and cation/anion ratio selection ensure meeting preferred trade-off solution between density, viscosity, melting point, and other physicochemical properties. A great role in the IL applications plays the azeotropic phenomena.

Considering a huge number of the "off the shelf" mixtures scheduled for destroying or recycling, it becomes key importance to develop the theoretically sound methods for reliable assessment of thermodynamic and phase behavior. Experimental retrieval of the azeotrope properties is time-consuming and a costly process. Availability of theoretical predictions for azeotropic phenomena would not only reduce this cost but also make efficient required experimental investigations.

The objective of this study is to present novel approach which encompasses global phase diagram technique and Pareto-optimal EoS parameter estimation for azeotropic and double azeotropic criteria evaluation in terms of critical parameters of pure components for the binary mixtures of refrigerants and ionic liquids.

This paper is organized as follows. In Section 2, the phase diagram classification and the one-fluid model of the equation of state for global phase diagrams are presented. Section 3 provides approach to sustainable property calculation based on a fuzzy set methodology providing a trade-off solution among different sources of data required for regression of model parameters. Section 4 discusses the results of azeotrope-breaking criteria for IL-refrigerant mixtures based at the approaches provided in previous sections.

2. Phase diagram classes and global phase diagram

Mapping of the global equilibrium surface into the parameter space of the equation of state model provides the most comprehensive set of criteria for prediction phase behavior of the binary mixture.

The impact of critical parameters of components on phase topology is provided via global phase diagrams. The diagrams are depicted in the space of the equation of state parameters, e.g., van der Waals a and b parameters. The specific points and lines of global phase diagrams, including tricritical points, double critical endpoints, azeotropic lines, etc., create the boundaries at the diagram and divide the model parameter space into the regions corresponding to the various types of the phase behavior. Generally, global phase diagram is expressed in dimensionless parameters which depend on the equation of state model. The global phase diagrams of such different models as the one-fluid EoS of binary Lennard-Jones fluid [6, 7] and the Redlich-Kwong model [5, 8, 9] are almost identical, in particular for the case of equal-sized molecules.

We consider here the cubic-type models:

$$p = \frac{\mathrm{RT}}{v-b} - \frac{a(T)}{v(v+b)} \tag{1}$$

where R is the universal gas constant and the EoS parameters a and b of mixture depend on the mole fractions x_i and x_j of the components i and j and on the corresponding parameters a_{ij} and b_{ij} for different pairs of interacting molecules:

$$a = \sum_{i=1}^{2}\sum_{j=1}^{2} x_i x_j a_{\mathrm{ij}}\left(1-k_{\mathrm{ij}}\right),\ b = \sum_{i=1}^{2}\sum_{j=1}^{2} x_i x_j b_{\mathrm{ij}} \tag{2}$$

The convenient set of dimensionless parameters for the Redlich-Kwong model is as follows [13]:

$$Z_1 = \frac{d_{22} - d_{11}}{d_{22} + d_{11}},$$

$$Z_2 = \frac{d_{22} - 2d_{12} + d_{11}}{d_{22} + d_{11}}, \tag{3}$$

$$Z_3 = \frac{b_{22} - b_{11}}{b_{22} + b_{11}},$$

$$Z_4 = \frac{b_{22} - 2b_{12} + b_{11}}{b_{22} + b_{11}}$$

where.

$$d_{\rm ij} = \frac{T_{\rm ij} b_{\rm ij}}{b_{\rm ii} b_{\rm jj}},\quad T_{\rm ij} = \left(\frac{\Omega_b a_{\rm ij}}{R\Omega_a b_{\rm ij}}\right)^{23},\quad \Omega_a = \left[9\left(2^{13} - 1\right)\right]^{-1},\quad \Omega_b = \frac{2^{13} - 1}{3}.$$

In the case of the Redlich-Kwong (RK) model [13], the value Λ is given by

$$\Lambda = \frac{\Theta_b}{\Theta_{\rm ab}(\Theta_b - 1)^2} + \frac{1}{\Theta_b + 1} = 0.67312, \tag{4}$$

where $\Theta_{\rm ab} = \frac{\Omega_a}{\Omega_b}$, $\Theta_b = \frac{z_c}{\Omega_b}$. According to Eq. (4), the boundary between azeotropic and non-azeotropic states in Z_1–Z_2 plane at fixed values of Z_3 and Z_4 is a straight line. The values are equal to Ω_a = 0.42747, Ω_b = 0.08664, and Z_c = 0.333.

The combining rules for the binary interaction parameters are

$$a_{\rm ij} = \left(1 - k_{\rm ij}\right)\sqrt{a_{\rm ii} a_{\rm jj}},\qquad b_{\rm ij} = \left(1 - l_{\rm ij}\right)\frac{b_{\rm ii} + b_{\rm jj}}{2}. \tag{5}$$

where k_{ij} and l_{ij} are fitting coefficients in the Lorentz-Berthelot combining rule ($k_{ij} = l_{ij} = 0$).

The simplest boundary is a normal critical point when two fluid phases are becoming identical. Critical conditions are expressed in terms of the molar Gibbs energy derivatives in the following way:

$$\left(\frac{\partial^2 G}{\partial x^2}\right)_{p,T} = \left(\frac{\partial^3 G}{\partial x^3}\right)_{p,T} = 0. \tag{6}$$

Corresponding critical conditions for the composition-temperature-volume variables are

$$A_{\rm xx} - {\rm W}A_{\rm xV} = 0;$$

$$A_{\rm xxx} - 3{\rm W}A_{\rm xxV} + 3W^2 A_{\rm xVV} - 3W^3 A_{\rm VVV} = 0; \tag{7}$$

where A is the molar Helmholtz energy and.

$W = \frac{A_{\rm xx}}{A_{\rm VV}}$ and $A_{\rm mVnx} = \left(\frac{\partial^{n+m} A}{\partial x^n \partial V^m}\right)_T$ are the contracted notations for differentiation operation which can be solved for V_C and T_C at a given concentration x.

Global phase diagrams generated for Redlich-Kwong model is presented in **Figures 1** and 2.

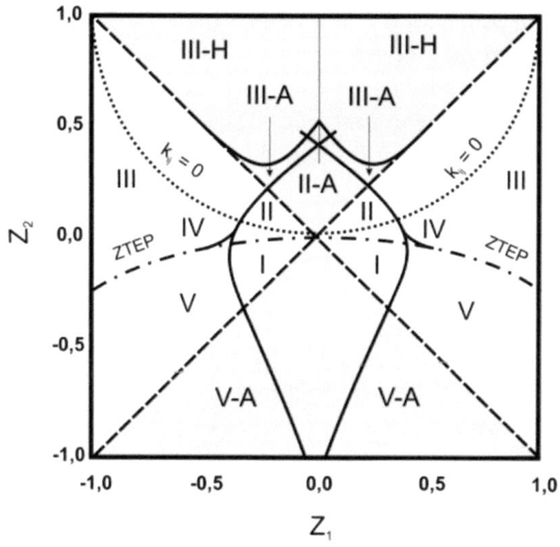

Figure 1.
Global phase diagram of the RK model [13], $Z_3 = Z_4 = 0$.

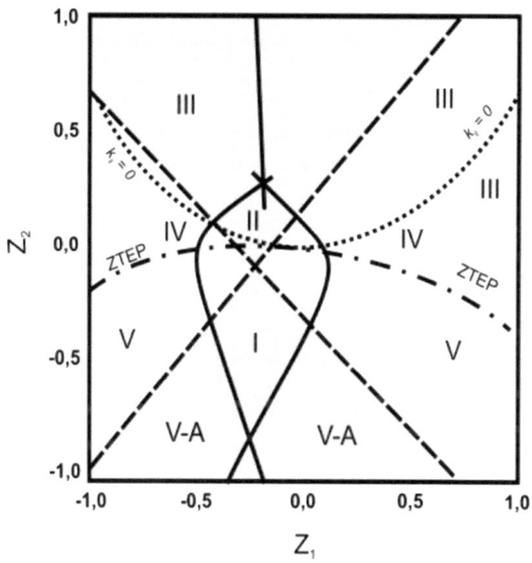

Figure 2.
Global phase diagram of the RK model [13], $Z_3 = Z_4 = 0.25$.

Here C_1 and C_2 are critical points of components 1 and 2; C_m is hypothetic critical point beyond solidification line. The types of phase behavior indicated as Roman numbers are described in [1–3].

3. Uncertainties and conflicts in the parameter estimation

Accounting the effects of uncertainty in the fluid-phase equilibria, modeling became important in the recent decade. Generally, the uncertainty tried to be resolved via probability and random process theories. However, the probabilistic methods can lead to the unreliable estimation of parameters. There are three main complimentary models of uncertainty described in literature:

- Convex models of uncertainty, developed by Ben-Haim and Elishakoff [15] as an extension of interval analysis

- Game-theoretic models of uncertainty deriving from *conflict* among the different goals (in our case, it is a conflict between thermodynamically inconsistent data)

- Verbal models of uncertainty deriving from *vagueness* and initiated to be resolved by Zadeh [14]

Three models of uncertainty cannot exist one by one in parameter estimation, and mathematical tools should reveal this fact. The conventional single-criterion methods of parameter estimation are examples of lopsided vision of multicriteria decision-making problem where only one set of variables, strongly dependent on decision-maker experience, is recommended. A lack of single meaning of optimality concept, following from the basics of modern game theory, points to impossibility to construct a completely formal algorithm for parameter estimation and futility of eliminating the uncertainty in the search process. It is more correct to consider the trade-off or rational parameters, which adequately describe thermodynamic properties and phase behavior, generated by EoS.

The following sequence of decision-making steps in model parameter estimation is proposed:

- Determination of the Pareto-optimal (or compromise or trade-off) set $\boldsymbol{X_P}$ as the formal solution of the multicriteria problem to minimize a conflict source of uncertainty

- Informal selection of convolution scheme to switch over a vector criterion $\boldsymbol{K}$ into a scalar combination of the Ki (X)

- Evaluation of the final decision vector $\boldsymbol{X_{opt}}$ $\boldsymbol{X_P}$ to minimize a vagueness source of uncertainty

3.1 Pareto set

The most important stage toward the multicriteria problem solving is an establishment of the Pareto domain X_P, i.e., such domain in model parameter space where it is not possible to reach a dominance of selected criteria over others. A geometrical visualization of the Pareto set (**AB** line) for the bi-criteria case in *2D* parameter space is given in **Figures 3** and **4**. For instance, the best least squares fit of the p–T-x phase equilibria data $K_1^{\min}$ usually does not correspond to the best data fit for critical line $K_2^{\max}$ and vice versa. Here $K_1^{\min}$ and $K_2^{\min}$ are the best or “ideal” solutions for each criterion found as a result of single-criterion optimization; for obviousness, parameters X_1 and X_2 could be interpreted as geometric and energetic parameters in the van der Waals EoS model.

To locate the Pareto set, we assume to compare two solutions, $\boldsymbol{X^*}$ and $\boldsymbol{X_0}$, which hold the inequality:

$$\boldsymbol{K}(\boldsymbol{X_0}) \leq \boldsymbol{K}(\boldsymbol{X}\ ). \tag{8}$$

It is obvious that $\boldsymbol{X_0}$ is preferable than $\boldsymbol{X^*}$. Thus, all $\boldsymbol{X^*}$ vectors satisfying Eq. (8) may be excluded. It is worth to analyze that only those $\boldsymbol{X^*}$ vectors for which

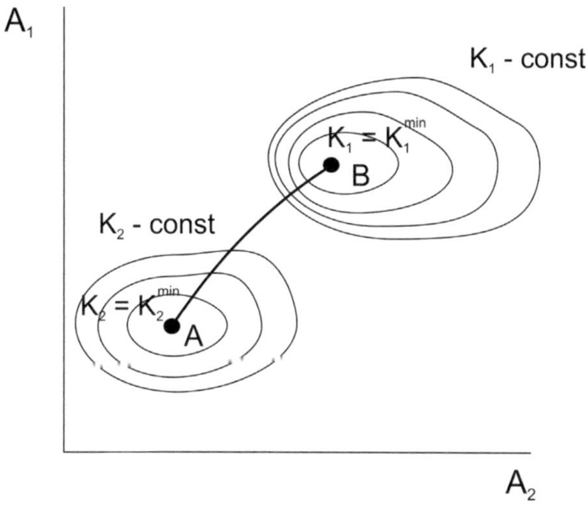

Figure 3.
The Pareto curve in criteria space.

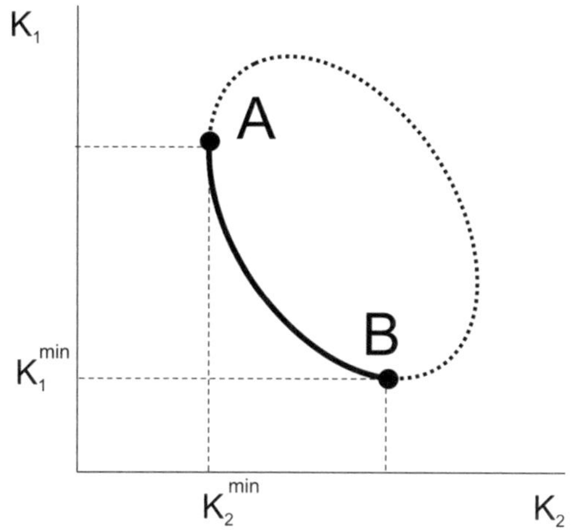

Figure 4.
The Pareto curve in parameter space.

there is no such X_O when for all criteria the inequality (8) is satisfied. The set of all values $X_P = X^*$ is the Pareto set, and the vector X_P is the unimprovable vector of the results, in case if from $K_i\ (X_O) \leq K_i\ (X_P)$ for any i it follows that $K\ (X_O) = K\ (X_P)$.

3.2 Crisp convolution schemes

Isolationistic and cooperative trends are usually considered for aggregation of local criteria vector into global scalar criterion. The isolationistic convolution schemes are additive, i.e., global criterion is represented as a weighted sum of local criteria and entropy as a sum of local criterion logarithms. If behavior of each criterion is complied with common decision to minimize some cooperative criterion, then a convolution scheme can be presented in the form

$$K_C(X) = \min\left[w_i\left(K_i(X) - K_i^0\right)\right], \qquad 1 \leq i \leq n, \quad X \in X_P, \tag{9}$$

where w_i are the weight coefficients, K_i^0 is an infimum of the desired result that is acceptable for decision-maker remaining in the coalition, and K_C is a global trade-off criterion. If it will be possible to come to an agreement about preference (weight) for each criterion, then the final decision can be found as a solution of scalar nonlinear programming problem:

$$K_C(X) = \min \sum_{i=1}^{n} \left| w_i \left(K_i(X) - K_i^0 \right) \right|, \quad \boldsymbol{X} \in \boldsymbol{X_P}. \tag{10}$$

In terms of game-theoretical approach, such coalition is defined as the von Neumann coalition scheme [16].

If no concordance among decision-makers is concerning the weight choice, then arbitration network is preferable. Classical arbitration scheme was derived mathematically rigorously by Nash but very often criticized from common sense [16]:

$$K_C(X) = \min \prod_{i=1}^{n} \left| K_i(X) - K_i^0 \right|, \quad \boldsymbol{X} \in \boldsymbol{X_P}. \tag{11}$$

All crisp convolution schemes under discussion try to reduce an uncertainty deriving from conflict among different criteria in the Pareto domain. The next step is extenuation of uncertainty driving from vagueness.

3.3 Fuzzy convolution scheme

Zadeh [14] put the theory of fuzzy sets forward with explicit reference to the vagueness of natural language, when describing quantitative or qualitative goals of the system. Here we assume that local criteria as well as different constraints in the ill-structured situation can be represented by fuzzy sets. A final decision is defined by the Bellman and Zadeh model [17] as the intersection of all fuzzy criteria and constraints and is represented by its membership function $\boldsymbol{\mu(X)}$ as follows:

$$\boldsymbol{\mu}(\boldsymbol{X}) = \boldsymbol{\mu_K}(\boldsymbol{X})\, \boldsymbol{\mu_C}(\boldsymbol{X}), \quad \boldsymbol{X} \in \boldsymbol{X_P}. \tag{12}$$

This problem is reduced to the standard nonlinear programming problems: to find the values $\boldsymbol{X}$ and λ that maximize λ that is subject to

$$\begin{aligned} &\lambda \leq \mu_{\mathrm{Ki}}(X), \quad i = 1, 2, \ldots, n; \\ &\lambda \leq \mu_{\mathrm{Cj}}(X), \quad j = 1, 2, \ldots, m \end{aligned} \tag{13}$$

Here, by way of illustration, the new approach was introduced to estimate the Redlich-Kwong EoS parameters for simultaneous description of the phase equilibria and critical line data in binary mixtures, thermodynamically consistent description of the inhomogeneous data, and other inconsistency problems arising in the modeling of phase equilibria.

3.4 Conflict between phase equilibria and critical line description in binary mixtures

Reliable models for thermodynamic and phase behavior description of binary mixtures are facing problems of adequate estimation of the binary interaction parameters from the restricted set of *VLE* data. In spite of availability of strict relationships to obtain from EoS model, the different derivatives of thermodynamic values, for instance, the prediction of critical lines from the EoS with parameters restored from *VLE* data, is questionable due to diverse sources of uncertainty in both the used models and experimental data.

For illustration, we consider thermodynamic and phase behavior of water-carbon dioxide system near the critical point of water. Experimental data on p-ρ-T-x properties have been taken from [18]; data on phase equilibria and critical curve have been extracted from [19, 20]. The critical lines have been calculated using algorithm developed in [21]. Phase equilibria calculations have been carried out with Michelsen and Mollerup method [22] for cubic EoS. We performed phase equilibria and critical line calculations for the RK EoS with binary interaction parameters k_{12} and l_{12} used in standard mixing rules

$$\begin{aligned} b &= b_{11}x^2 + l_{12}x(1-x)\left(\frac{b_{11}+b_{22}}{2}\right) + b_{22}(1-x)^2 \\ a &= a_{11}x^2 + k_{12}x(1-x)\sqrt{a_{11}a_{22}} + a_{22}(1-x)^2 \end{aligned} \tag{14}$$

and restored from different crisp convolution schemes. For simplicity, the results of calculation for phase equilibria and critical line are presented in **Figures 5** and **6** only for most selected compromise schemes. The challenge of conflict between parameters retrieved from different sections of thermodynamic surface remains important for practically all EoS including sophisticated multiparameter equation of

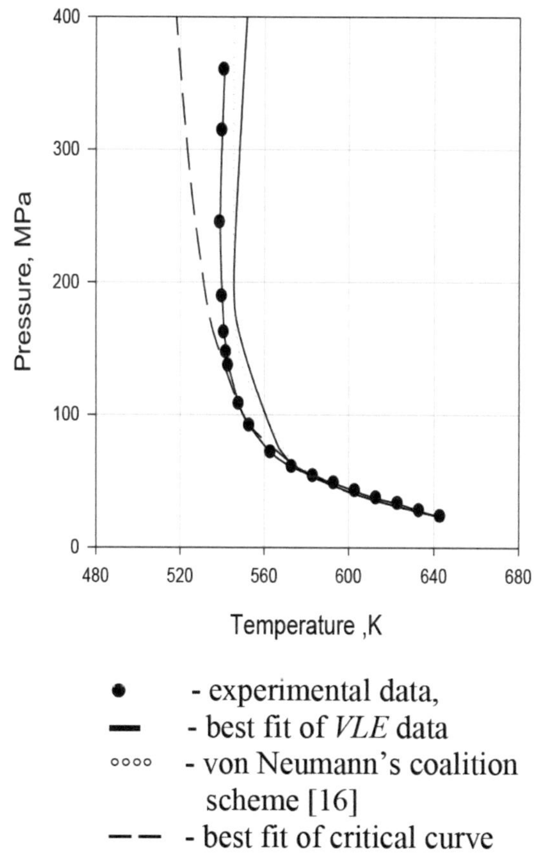

Figure 5.
Critical line of H_2O—CO_2 system [21]. • Experimental data — Best fit of VLE *data* ºººº *von Neumann's coalition scheme [16] — — Best fit of critical curve.*

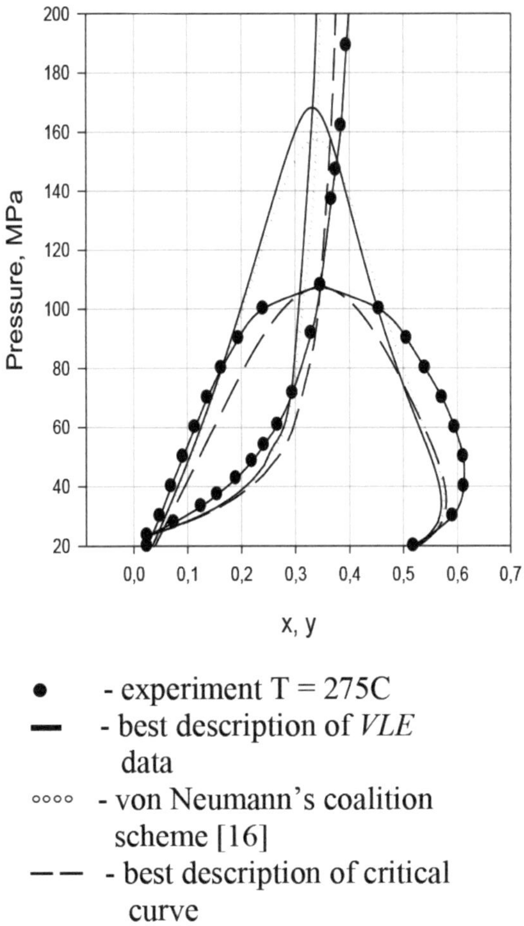

Figure 6.
Phase equilibria in H_2O—CO_2 system [20]. • Experiment T = 275C. ▬ Best description of VLE *data.* ºººº *von Neumann's coalition scheme [16]. — — Best description of critical curve.*

state. In general, the conflict can be described as follows: if interaction parameters are retrieved from the one class of properties, the prediction of other properties is doubtful in spite of validity of thermodynamic relationships. The final solution will depend on the problem setting and decision-maker subjective experience.

4. Results and discussion

This study provides a novel approach for defining the quantifiable estimation of boundary states and specific points which define changes of phase behavior. The global phase diagram technique is applied for deriving the analytical expressions and Pareto-based approach with fuzzy convolution scheme used for adequate evaluation of model parameters.

There are no rigorous mathematical methods to construct adequate model without subjectively based solution due to a number of uncertainties and conflicts. To reduce the source of unavoidable uncertainty, the different compromise schemes of criteria convolution are considered. It is important to note that the selection of the convolution scheme is a subjective choice of the decision-maker.

Below we provide results and discussion of application of the abovementioned approach for identification of the azeotrope- and double azeotrope-breaking criteria for imidazolium (IL)-based ionic liquids and industrial refrigerant mixtures. IL doping leads to the breaking of azeotrope in binary refrigerant mixtures that open the way for the azeotrope refrigerant mixture separation technologies in order to remove the environmentally harmful substances.

4.1 Azeotrope-breaking criteria

Applying the cubic model of the equation of state, only the critical properties and acentric factor of the individual components in mixtures are sufficient to define the phase behavior in the interested sector of the parameters.

The degenerated critical azeotrope point is a boundary state separating azeotrope and non-azeotrope and produces the limit of the critical azeotrope at $x_i \to 0$ or at $x_i \to 1$. The solution of the thermodynamic equation system for a degenerated critical azeotrope [5–7, 9]

$$\left(\frac{\partial p}{\partial V}\right)_{T,x} = \left(\frac{\partial^2 p}{\partial V^2}\right)_{T,x} = \left(\frac{\partial p}{\partial x}\right)_{T,V} = 0 \tag{15}$$

gives the following relationship for dimensionless parameters Z_i:

$$Z_2 = \mp Z_1 - (1 \pm Z_1)\left(\frac{1 - Z_4}{1 \pm Z_3} - 1\right)\Lambda, \tag{16}$$

where the upper signs + or − correspond to $x_2 = 0$ and the lower signs - to $x_2 = 1$, respectively.

To define the azeotropic states, the parameters Z_i can be expressed via critical (pseudocritical) temperatures T_{ci} and pressures P_{ci} of pure components and empirical binary interaction parameters k_{12} and l_{12} (17). The unlike pair interaction parameters Z_2 and Z_4 (i.e., a_{12} and b_{12}) can be estimated solving simultaneously the system of Eqs. (17) for the given Z_1 and Z_3 (or the set of pure component constants a_{11}, b_{11}, a_{22}, b_{22}) that are determined from the critical parameters of the components:

$$\begin{gathered} Z_1 = \frac{T_{c2}^2/P_{c2} - T_{c1}^2/P_{c1}}{T_{c2}^2/P_{c2} + T_{c1}^2/P_{c1}},\ Z_2 = \frac{T_{c2}^2/P_{c2} - 2(1-k_{12})\frac{T_{c1}T_{c2}}{\sqrt{P_{c1}P_{c2}}} + T_{c1}^2/P_{c1}}{T_{c2}^2/P_{c2} + T_{c1}^2/P_{c1}}, \\ Z_3 = \frac{T_{c2}/P_{c2} - T_{c1}/P_{c1}}{T_{c2}/P_{c2} + T_{c1}/P_{c1}}, \\ Z_4 = \frac{T_{c1}/P_{c1} - (1-l_{12})(T_{c1}/P_{c1} + T_{c2}/P_{c2}) + T_{c2}/P_{c2}}{T_{c2}/P_{c2} + T_{c1}/P_{c1}}. \end{gathered} \tag{17}$$

The boundary between azeotrope and zeotrope states in Z_1–Z_2 plane at fixed values of Z_3 and Z_4 is a straight line. The definition of azeotropic and zeotropic states for refrigerants is depicted in **Figure** 7.

4.2 Double azeotrope-breaking criterion

Double azeotropic phenomena can be observed in the global phase diagram only in the vicinity of the crossing point of two straight azeotropic borders in (Z_1, Z_2) plane (**Figures 8** and **9**):

$$Z_{2i} = \frac{\Psi^+ - \Psi^-}{2 + \Psi^+ + \Psi^-},\ Z_1^i = \frac{\Psi^+ + \Psi^-}{2 + \Psi^+ + \Psi^-},\ \text{where } \Psi^\pm = \left(\frac{1 - Z_4}{1 \pm Z_3} - 1\right)\Lambda. \tag{18}$$

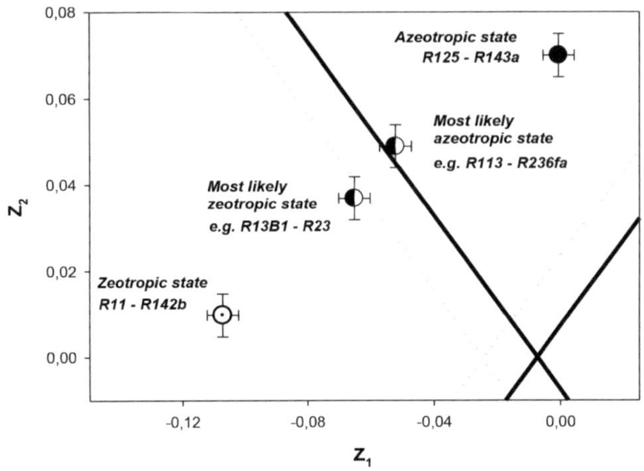

Figure 7.
Azeotropic boundaries and their position in the global phase diagram. • R507 (R125/R143a)—position in azeotropic sector ($Z_1 = -0.54\ 10^{-4}$; $Z_2 = 0.07$; $Z_3 = -0.01$; $Z_4 = 0$). —— Azeotropic boundaries for R125/R143a mixture ($Z_3 = -0.01$; $Z_4 = 0$). ʘ R11/R142b—position in zeotropic sector ($Z_1 = -0.11$; $Z_2 = 0.97\ 10^{-3}$; $Z_3 = -0.035$; $Z_4 = 0$). .... Azeotropic boundaries for R11/142b mixture ($Z_3 = -0.035$; $Z_4 = 0$).

The best results were demonstrated by application of the Schwarzentruber-Renon and Wang-Sandler mixing rule [10] with three adjustable parameters (**Figure 8**). The use of local mapping shows good results of double azeotropic description at 323.05 K using the standard mixing rule (**Figure 8**).

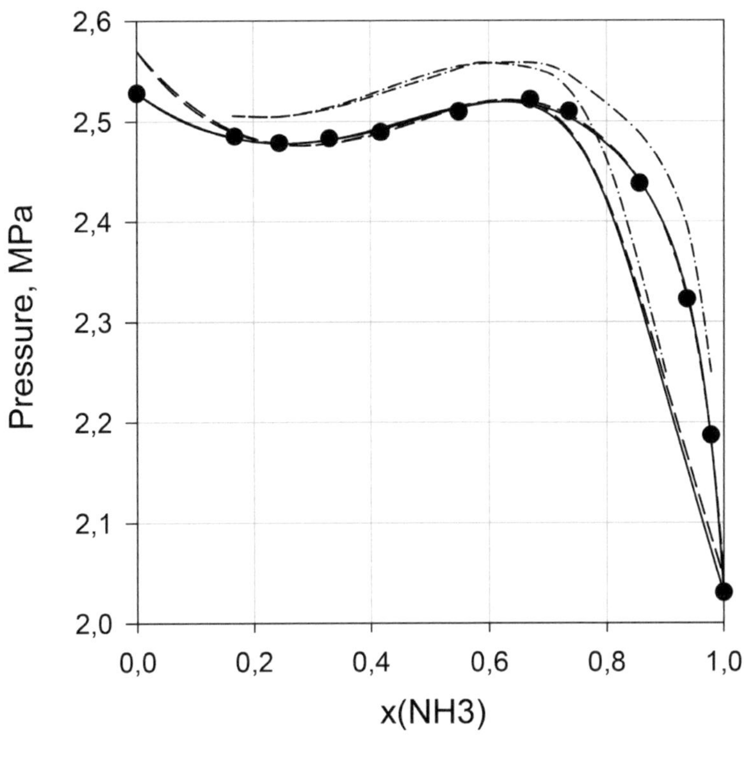

Figure 8.
Phase diagrams for R717-R125 mixture at 323.05 K. Schwarzentruber-Renon mixing rule [23].

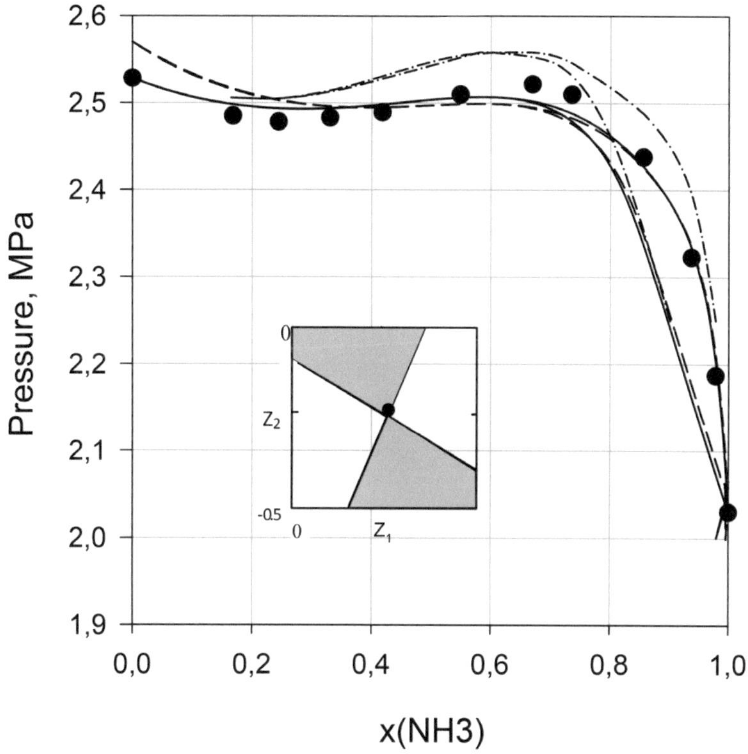

Figure 9.
Phase diagrams for R717-R125 mixture at 323.05 K. Standard mixing rule [24]. A double azeotrope near the crossing point of the two straight azeotropic borders in (Z_1, Z_2) plane. • Experimental data [23, 24]. ● Local mapping approach [10]. — · — equation of state approach. ——— model [27].

4.3 Applications of ionic liquids in azeotrope mixture distillation

The set of parameters for a given equation of state model univocally defines a global phase diagram and, consequently, evolution of phase behavior for binary mixture in a wide range of temperatures and pressures. Global phase diagram for model systems of components explores that binary mixture of industrial refrigerants with imidazolium (IL)-based ionic liquids does not experience azeotropic behavior in the practicable range of parameters.

Distribution of critical points for major components of refrigerants [25–29] and hypothetical critical parameters of a number of imidazole-based ionic liquids is depicted in **Figure 10**.

It shall be noted that at subcritical temperatures, IL may undergo thermal decomposition that causes uncertainty in assessment of critical parameters. Usually, the available values of critical points of ionic liquids are derived from low-temperature regions having extremely small saturation pressures. Computational procedures for finding model parameters are unstable. This can lead to errors in the predictions of phase equilibria at high temperatures.

Thanks to undetectable vapor pressure, ILs are considered as potential environmentally friendly candidates for replacing conventional solvents. The selective solubility properties of the ILs appeared for particular components of the mixtures and can be treated as extraction media for separation processes. Moreover, the increase of efficiency for absorption processes is promoted thanks to nonvolatile feature of ionic liquids acting as absorbents.

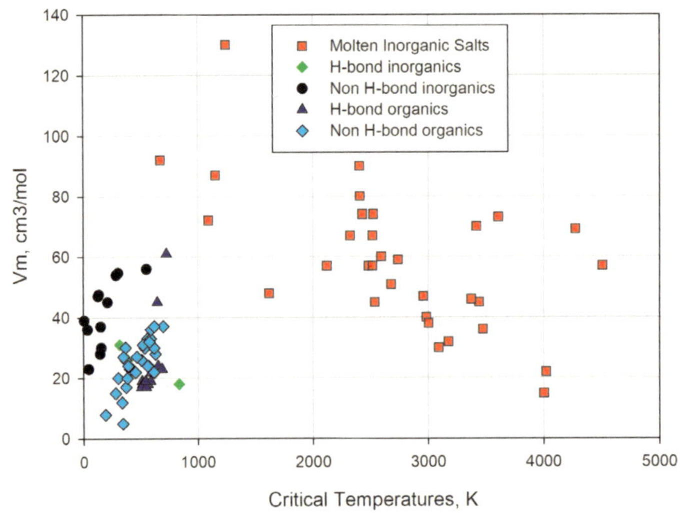

Figure 10.
Critical point temperatures and molar volumes of representative components from [25–29].

The information on breaking of azeotrope is crucial for the separation of different industrial mixtures and is intensively discussed in the literature. The proposed existing expressions for identification of azeotrope behavior generally are empirical.

To describe and predict the phase behavior of the mixture, the equation of state models is more suitable for calculation of the thermodynamic properties.

The calculations of phase equilibria for system imidazolium-based ionic liquid and refrigerants R134a and R1234yf are performed. The Redlich-Kwong one-fluid model equation of state was selected due to simplicity, few parameters to be estimated, existing robust computational algorithms for obtaining the derivations of different thermodynamic features, as well as a large amount of existing data on binary interacting parameters in the existing literature.

The phase behavior of imidazolium-based ionic liquids $C_8H_{11}N_3F_6S_2O_4$ ([EMIm][Tf2N]) and $C_{10}H_{19}N_2BF_4$ ([HMIm][BF_4]) with refrigerants R134a and R1234yf was evaluated using the parameters regressed at the low-pressure experimental data. It is noted that the variation of anionic group leads to the shift of critical point of ILs and obviously impact intermolecular interactions between ionic liquids and molecules of refrigerants. To this end the phase behavior pattern is also impacted. Variation in the k_{12} interaction coefficient shifts the position of a specific point on the global phase diagram. For R1234yf-[HMIm][BF_4] system, the position of the specific point at different values $k_{12} = -0.1, 0, +0.1$ demonstrates a tendency to transition from azeotrope to zeotrope state or vice versa. The binary interaction parameters k_{12} and l_{12} for R134a-Il blends were restored from experimental data provided by Ren et al. [28, 29] with Pareto-based method described in Section 3.

In case a specific point is located in the northern or southern quadrants of the diagrams depicted in **Figure 11**, the azeotropic phenomenon is expected to appear in the binary mixture. The pattern of specific point location for ionic liquid [HMIm][BF_4] + refrigerants R134a (R1234yf) systems is also provided in **Figure 11**.

It is considered that the azeotrope definitely appears in the R134a-R1234yf system. The literature search provides lack of experimental data for this system. The boundaries presented in **Figure 11** for the R1234yf-[HMIm][BF_4] mixture practically coincide. The addition of the ionic liquid to azeotropic mixture leads to azeotrope-breaking that is demonstrated by a change of phase envelope for the R134a-R1234yf-[HMIm][BF_4] mixture in **Figure 12**.

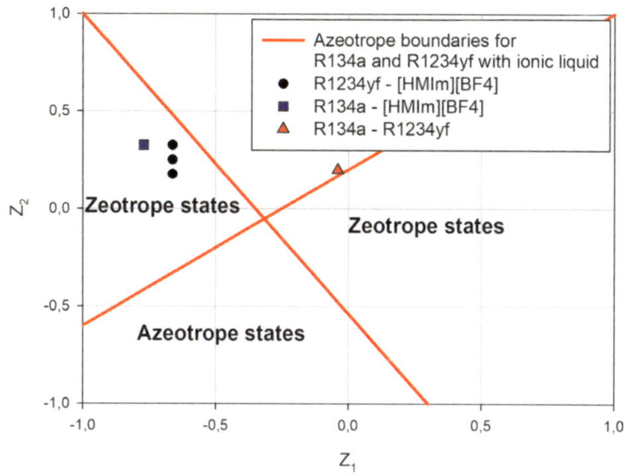

Figure 11.
Allocation of characteristics points on the global phase diagram for R134a-R1234yf mixture with ionic liquids.

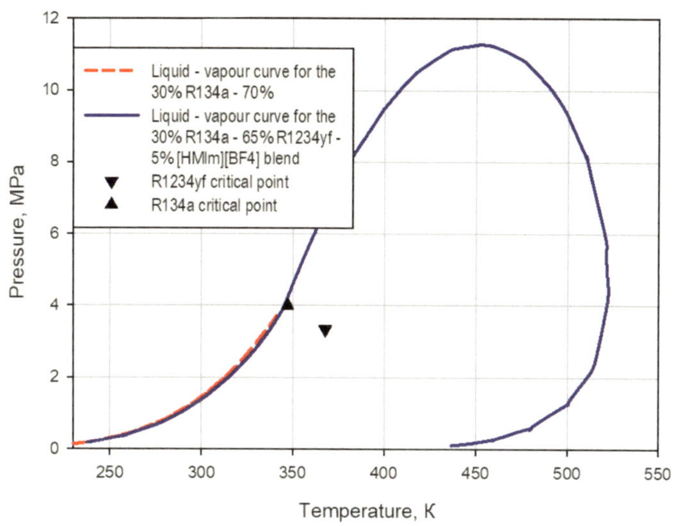

Figure 12.
Azeotrope-breaking in the R134a-R1234yf mixture at ionic liquid addition.

Positive value of binary interaction coefficient k_{12} can report on III-type of phase behavior for the system studied. The calculations were performed in MATLAB software on the base of the algorithms proposed by Michelsen-Mollerup [23].

5. Conclusions

The responses to the environmental challenges require development and application of new environmentally friendly working media. As one of the promising media for chemical and refrigeration industry, the mixtures of conventional refrigerants with ionic liquids are considered. This requires reliable data on thermophysical properties and phase behavior of the mixture.

Tremendously growing amount of data and development of the data science provides new basis for estimation of the model parameters which influence the description and further prediction of the different physical processes.

In this study we present new approach which does not require vapor–liquid equilibrium calculations for binary mixtures. This approach is based on synergetic combination of global phase diagram technique and Pareto-based regression to reduce the uncertainty level caused by different sources of the data.

The global phase diagram is used to determine the type of phase behavior and derive analytical expressions to predict azeotrope and double azeotrope phenomena in terms of critical parameters of pure components.

To restore the EoS model parameters under uncertainty, the Pareto-optimality concept with fuzzy convolution scheme is applied. This approach is quite general and can be applied to other mathematical models, which describe a wide spectrum of phenomena of thermodynamic and phase behavior.

The azeotrope and double azeotrope criteria were elaborated and assessed for the imidazolium (IL)-based ionic liquids and industrial refrigerant mixtures. It was shown that IL doping leads to the breaking of azeotrope in binary refrigerant mixtures that open the way for the azeotrope refrigerant mixture separation technologies in order to remove the environmentally harmful substances.

The azeotrope phenomena in the refrigerant-IL mixtures are discussed, and conclusion about the highly improbable azeotrope blend formation for these systems is given. Azeotrope-breaking in the R134a-R1234yf mixture at IL doping is considered as an illustration of zeotrope behavior in the refrigerant-IL mixtures. Global phase behavior of ionic liquid-industrial refrigerant mixture is analyzed, and possible types of phase behavior according to the classification scheme of Scott and Van Konynenburg are established.

Author details

Sergey Artemenko and Victor Mazur*
Institute of Refrigeration, Cryotechnologies, and Eco-Power Engineering of Odessa National Academy of Food Technologies, Odessa, Ukraine

*Address all correspondence to: victor.mazur@gmail.com

References

[1] Van Konynenburg P, Scott R. Critical lines and phase equilibria in binary van der Waals mixtures. Philosophical Transactions of the Royal Society of London, Series A: Mathematical, Physical and Engineering Sciences. 1980;**298**:495-540. DOI: 10.1098/rsta.1980.0266

[2] Varchenko A. Theorems on the topological equisingularity of families of algebraic varieties and families of polynomial mappings. Izvestija Akademii Nauk SSSR Seriya Matematicheskaya. 1972;**36**(5): 957-1019. DOI: 10.1070/IM1972v006n05ABEH001909

[3] Aicardi F, Valentin P, Ferrand E. On the classification of generic phenomena in one-parameter families of thermodynamic binary mixtures. Physical Chemistry Chemical Physics. 2002;**4**:884-895. DOI: 10.1039/B109105K

[4] Furman D, Dattagupta S, Griffiths RB. Global phase diagram for a three-component model. Physics Review. 1977;**B15**:441. DOI: 10.1103/PhysRevB.15.441

[5] Deiters UK, Kraska T. High-Pressure Fluid Phase Equilibria: Phenomenology and Computation. Netherlands: Elsevier; 2018. p. 370. ISBN: 9780444563545

[6] Mazur V, Boshkov LV, Murakhovsky R. Global phase behavior in binary Lennard–Jones mixtures. Physics Letters. 1984;**104A**:415-418. DOI: 10.1016/0375-9601(84)90746-1

[7] Boshkov L, Mazur V. Phase behaviour of the two-component Lennard-Jones fluid, high-temperature. Thermophysics. 1989;**1**:641-643. (in Russian)

[8] Deiters UK, Pegg IL. Systematic investigation of the phase behaviour in binary fluid mixtures. I. Calculations based on the Redlich-Kwong equation of state. The Journal of Chemical Physics. 1989;**90**:6632-6641. DOI: 10.1063/1.456280

[9] Kolafa J. Azeotropic phenomena in the global phase diagram of the Redlich-Kwong equation of state. Physical Chemistry Chemical Physics. 1999;**1**: 5665-5670

[10] Artemenko S, Mazur V. Azeotropic in the natural and synthetic refrigerant mixtures. International Journal of Refrigeration. 2007, 2007;**30**:831-840. DOI: 10.1016/j.ijrefrig.2006.11.010

[11] Aslam N, Sunol AK. Computing all the azeotropes in refrigerant mixtures through equations of state. Fluid Phase Equilibria. 2004;**224**:97-109. DOI: 10.1016/j.fluid.2004.03.014

[12] Patel K, Sunol A. Automatic generation of global phase equilibrium diagrams for binary systems from equations of state. Computers and Chemical Engineering. 2009;**3**:1793. DOI: 10.1016/j.compchemeng.2009.03.004

[13] Redlich O, Kwong JNS. On the Thermodynamics of Solutions. Chemical Reviews. 1949;**44**:233-244. DOI: 10.1021/cr60137a013

[14] Zadeh L. Fuzzy Sets. Information and Control. 1965;**8**:338-353. DOI: 10.1016/S0019-9958(65)90241-X

[15] Ben-Haim Y, Elishakoff I. Convex Models of Uncertainty in Applied Mechanics. Studies in Applied Mechanic s (25) Tribology Series (25). Amsterdam: Elsevier; 1990. p. 221. ISBN: 0444417583, 9780444417589

[16] Von Neumann-Morgenstern Stable Sets. Handbook of Game Theory with

Economic Applications. Netherlands: Elsevier; 1992;**1**:543-590. DOI: 10.1016/S1574-0005(05)80020-7

[17] Bellman RE, Zadeh LA. Decision making in a fuzzy environment. Management Science. 1970;**17**:141-164. Available from: https://www.jstor.org/stable/2629367

[18] Span R, Wagner W. A new equation of state for carbon dioxide covering the fluid region from the triple point temperature to 1100K at pressures up to 800 MPa. Journal of Physical and Chemical Reference Data. 1996;**25**: 1509-1596. DOI: 10.1063/1.555991

[19] Mather A, Franck E. Phase equilibria in the system carbon dioxide —Water at elevated pressures. The Journal of Physical Chemistry. 1992;**6**: 6-8. DOI: 10.1021/j100180a003

[20] Todheide K, Frank E. Das zweiphasengebiet und die kritische kurve im system kohlendioxid—Wasser bis zu drucken von 3500 bar. Zeitschrift fur Physikalische Chemie (Neue Folge). 1963;**37**:387-401. DOI: 10.1524/zpch.1963.37.5_6.387

[21] Heidemann R, Khalil A. The calculation of critical points. AICHE Journal. 1980;**26**:769-778. DOI: 10.1002/aic.690260510

[22] Michelsen L, Mollerup J. Thermodynamic Models, Fundamentals and Computational Aspects. Denmark: Lyngby; 2002

[23] Schwarzentruber J, Renon H. Extension of UNIFAC to high pressures and temperatures by the use of a cubic equation of state. Industrial and Engineering Chemistry Research. 1989; **289**:1049-1055. DOI: 10.1021/ie00091a026

[24] Shiflett MB, Sandler SI. Modeling fluorocarbon vapour liquid equilibria using the Wonge-Sandler model. Fluid Phase Equilibria. 1998;**147**:145-162. DOI: 10.1016/S0378-3812(98)00253-2

[25] Janz GJ. NIST Properties of Molten Salts Database, NIST SRD 27, Version 2.0. NY, USA: NIST; 1992

[26] Lemmon E, Huber M, McLinden M. NIST Reference Fluid Thermodynamic and Transport Properties—REFPROP. Version 9.1. Boulder: NIST; 2013

[27] Pereiro AB, Araujo JMM, Esperanca JMSS, Marrucho IM, Rebelo LPN. Ionic liquids in separations of azeotropic systems—A review. The Journal of Chemical Thermodynamics. 2012;**46**: 2-28. DOI: 10.1016/j.jct.2011.05.026

[28] Ren W, Scurto A. Phase equilibria of imidazolium ionic liquids and the refrigerant gas, 1,1,1,2-tetrafluoroethane (R-134a). Fluid Phase Equilibria. 2009;**286**(1):1-7. DOI: 10.1016/j.fluid.2009.07.007

[29] Ren W, Scurto A, Mark B, Shiflett M, Yokozeki A. Phase behavior and equilibria of ionic liquids and refrigerants: 1-Ethyl-3-methyl-imidazolium Bis (trifluoromethylsulfonyl) imide ([EMIm] [Tf 2 N]) and R-134a. ACS Symposium Se ries. 2009;**1006**:112-128. DOI: 10.1021/bk-2009-1006.ch006

Section 4

Reactive Distillation

Chapter 6

Reactive Distillation: Modeling, Simulation, and Optimization

Vandana Sakhre

Abstract

Chemical process industries deal with production which further utilizes reaction followed by separation of the reaction mixtures. Reactive distillation is a new technique of combination of both reaction and separation in a single unit beneficial for equilibrium-limited reactions and also cost-effective. This makes it a highly complex process because many parameters involved in both reaction and separation are interactive in nature. In this chapter, modeling, simulation, and optimization of reactive distillation are presented. Methyl acetate production via reactive distillation is chosen as a case study. The results are compared for both experimental and simulation studies. The synthesis of methyl acetate was carried out in a packed RDC by catalytic esterification using acetic acid and methanol as reactants in a pilot-scale experimental setup. A strong acidic ion exchange catalyst, Amberlyst-15, was used to enhance the rate of heterogeneous esterification reaction. The result obtained was observed with change in various variables including the reflux ratio (RR), distillate-to-feed (D/F) ratio, and bottom-to-feed (B/F) ratio with respect to product composition. The optimization and sensitivity analysis was carried out using Aspen Plus process simulation software.

Keywords: modeling, reactive distillation, optimization, simulation

1. Introduction

1.1 Reactive distillation (RD)

Chemical engineering deals with the conversion of raw material into products via a chemical unit process or unit operations. Manufacturing of various chemicals like esters, ethers, cumene, petroleum processing unit, etc. required a reactor followed by separator such as a distillation unit to separate the required product from other constituents on the basis of relative volatility [1]. There are various constraints on this type of processing like more space required for the installation of the unit, higher cost, more energy input requirement, and reduced selectivity. Specifically the conversion limits for reversible reactions are difficult to overcome toward highest purity of product because once the equilibrium is achieved in the system, no more reactant will be converted into products. In view of all these constraints, reactive distillation emerged as a novel technique of process intensification in which reaction and separation of product take place simultaneously in a single column [2].

IntechOpen

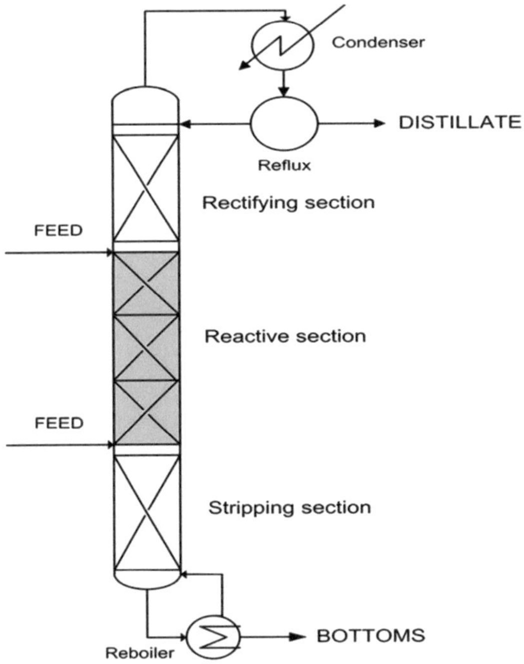

Figure 1.
Schematic diagram of reactive distillation column (RDC).

In the case of reactive distillation, total capital cost is reduced due to two combined process steps held in the single unit. This kind of integration is also beneficial in reducing pump cost and other instrumentation cost. The saving in total energy cost is due to exothermic nature of many chemical reactions which in turn are beneficial in providing heat for separation of components simultaneously [3–10]. The schematic diagram of reactive distillation column is shown in **Figure 1**.

2. Industrial application of reactive distillation

Reactive distillation, which uses heterogeneous catalysts known as catalytic distillation, was firstly considered for RD [11], but it then remained uninvestigated and lacked research interests until the 1980s. However in 1980, with the advent of reactive distillation technology, Eastman Company tentatively carried out synthesis of high-purity methyl acetate. Later on RD was categorized as hybrid and non-hybrid columns [12, 13]. Hybrid RD is used to describe columns, which have separate reactive and separation sections, while the reaction takes place in the whole non-hybrid RD column.

After the success story of Eastman Company, several European countries and universities joined forces to work on a development strategy for reactive distillation process under the umbrella of Brite Euram project. Sulzer Chemtech has developed special structured catalytic packing for reactive distillation columns [14]. RD is an important method for many chemical syntheses which require recovery of chemicals such as recovery of acetic acid. RD uses cation-exchange resin for many liquid-phase homogeneous catalyst reactions such as butyl acetate synthesis and helps in separating catalyst during downstream processing. The investigation of many such reactions is reported [15–17]. Transesterification for synthesis and characterization of biodiesel from different raw material such as palm oil, mustard oil, etc. has been proposed but still not commercialized using various

Process	Industrial location
Synthesis of acetates	Europe
Hydrolysis of methyl acetate	Europe and Asia
Synthesis of methylal	Europe and Asia
Removal of methanol from formaldehyde	Europe
Fatty acid ester	Asia

Table 1.
Commercial application of reactive distillation.

homogeneous and heterogeneous catalysts. However, hydrodesulfurization of light oil fractions has been carried out commercially for diesel deep hydrodesulfurization.

CDTECH, the major commercial process technology provider, licensed up to now over 200 commercial-scale processes. Sulzer reports the commercial application of reactive distillation as synthesis of ethyl, methyl, and butyl acetate, hydrolysis of methyl acetate, synthesis of methylal, removal of methanol from formaldehyde, and formation of fatty acid esters. Commercial reactive distillation application with Katapak licensed from Sulzer is tabulated in **Table 1**.

3. Industrial perspective of reactive distillation

Reactive distillation (RD) is a hybrid combination of reaction and separation in a single vessel. The first patent for this process route was out in the 1920s, but little was carried out till 1980 by the Eastman Company who synthesized methyl acetate for the first time using this technique. The following reactions have shown potential for reactive distillation:

3.1 Esterification

In esterification reaction, alcohol and acid react to form an ester. Esters are chemical compounds having pleasant fruity odor.

$$ROOR' + NaOH \rightarrow ROONa + HOR'$$

The main application of esters is in the synthesis of artificial flavor and essence and solvent for oil, gum, fat, and resins. They are also used as plasticizers. Esterification is the oldest reaction carried out in a reactive distillation column. For example, in conventional methyl acetate production, the yield of methyl acetate is low because of low boiling azeotrope formation. This constraint is removed in RD and almost pure methyl acetate can be collected. Fatty acid esters are natural chemicals used, among other things in cosmetics; plastics and surfactants were also reported to be synthesized in reactive distillation.

3.2 Transesterification

Transesterification reaction in general can be represented as the reaction between triglyceride and alcohol to produce alkyl esters and glycerol. The best example is a synthesis of biodiesel using transesterification. Commercially, no industrial unit has been reported on synthesis of biodiesel in RD, but the literature shows that pilot-scale synthesis is possible. This process occurs by reacting the vegetable oil with alcohol in the presence of an alkaline or acidic catalyst.

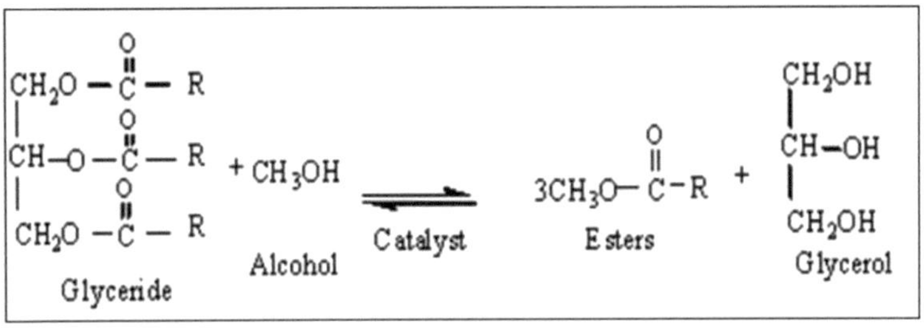

Heterogeneous catalysts are more effective from an economical point of view for biodiesel production. Sometimes transesterification can be a beneficial alternative to hydrolysis as it does not involve formation of water, and moreover, it brings out the value added through formation of another ester.

3.3 Etherification

Etherification refers to the synthesis of ethers from alcohol and acid. Ethers are an indispensable part of the fuel industry as, like the properties of alcohol, ether also enhances the octane value of fuel when added in appropriate proportion. Several model reactions via RD such as MTBE, ETBE, and TAME have been studied since last two decades. These fuel oxygenates are formed by reaction of isobutylene with alcohol to give ether and water. However, another alternative is to react tert-amyl alcohol (TAA) with corresponding lower alcohol such as methanol or ethanol.

$$\text{Alcohol} + \text{Isobutylene} \rightarrow \text{Ether}$$

$$\text{Ex : for MTBE : } CH_3OH + (CH_3)_2CCH_2 \rightarrow CH_3OC\,(CH_3)_3$$

$$\text{For ETBE : } CH_3CH_2CH_3 + C_2H_5OH \rightarrow (CH_3)_3OC_2H_5$$

3.4 Alkylation

Transfer of alkyl group from one molecule to another is known as alkylation. Cumene and ethyl benzene are some examples which are synthesized using alkylation process. In this process alkanes, which are a part of paraffin compounds, are reacted with an aromatic compound which results in production of a high-quality fuel substitutes like cumene. These compounds are added to gasoline as a blend to improve its octane number, reduce the engine problems like gum deposits on oxidation, etc. High aviation fuel blends are produced using an alkylation process whose octane number is denoted by a performance number having a value of greater than 100. The catalytic alkylation method uses aluminum chloride and hydrochloric acid as catalyst to initiate the reaction between benzene and propylene.

3.5 Aldol condensation

In an aldol condensation, an enolate ion reacts with a carbonyl compound to form a β-hydroxyaldehyde or β-hydroxyketone, followed by a dehydration to give a conjugated enone. By using reactive distillation (RD), one can improve the selectivity toward the intermediate or final product depending on the type of catalyst used and by continuously removing the desired product from the reaction zone.

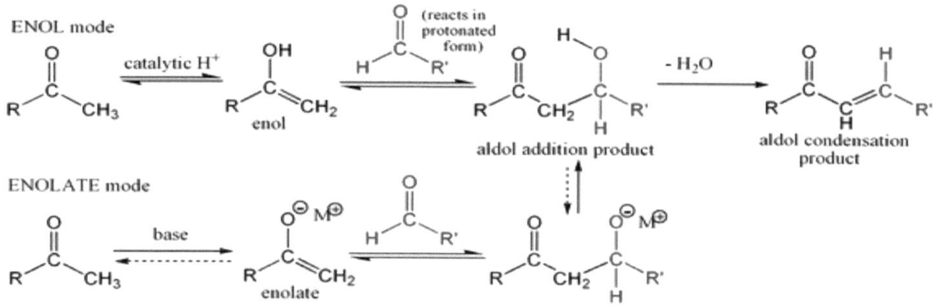

3.6 Dehydration

Dehydration reaction simply means removal of water. This process is employed generally for glycerol to obtain acetol. This reaction is usually carried into the presence of various metallic catalysts like alumina, magnesium, ruthenium, nickel, platinum, palladium, copper, Raney nickel, etc. Single-stage and two-stage reactive distillation techniques are being employed, and special care is being taken to regenerate these catalysts as they are classified as precious and non-precious catalysts.

3.7 Acetylation

Various processes thereby produce a by-product which is of other important industrial use. Like in the case of biodiesel manufacturing using methanol, we get a secondary by-product called glycerol. It is a very good raw material for the process called acetylating as in this process, especially when carried out in reactive distillation column, it is reported that about 99% conversion of glycerol into triacetin is observed. This triacetin acts as an additive in compression engine fuels and reduced the knocking in the engine.

3.8 Isomerization

Isomerization is a process in which one molecule is transformed into another molecule which has exactly the same atom, but they have different arrangements. A-isophorone and b-isophorone in spite of being isomers can be very well separated by reactive distillation as there is a large difference in their volatilities.

3.9 Oligomerization

Oligomerization is a chemical process that converts monomers to macromolecular complexes through a finite degree of polymerization. Oligomer esters and acid were hydrolyzed using RD technology, and the results were consistent with industrial literature.

3.10 Product purity

Product purity is an ultimate customer requirement. If these are not fulfilled or low-quality product is supplied to the customer, the expectation of the customer will not be fulfilled. For this reason, quality parameters need to be defined. These parameters are differing in different cases. For example, few quality indexes like physical and chemical characteristics of the product, medicinal effects, toxicity, and shelf life are required to be given in the case of pharmaceutical products. Quality indexes such as taste, nutritional properties, texture, etc. are important in the case of food products. Similarly for products from chemical processes, final composition or product purity as quality index is required.

4. Importance of product purity in chemical engineering

Synthesis of various chemicals usually is carried out in a reactor which may or may not be followed by separator. Either the case may be choice of design variable is very important. The market value of overhead product or the bottom product relies on its purity. Also the need of any further treatment for enhancing the purity relies on the initial product composition. In view of this, the degree of freedom for the column should be zero; that means the number of variables should be the same or equal to the number of equations involved in modeling. For example for a distillation column, if a designer specifies reflux ratio or boil up ratio and a distillate rate, then there will be corresponding unique set of distillate and bottom composition with respect to a fixed feed flow rate.

5. Product purity in reactive distillation

Variability in the product purity is due to various factors including variable flow rate, reboiler heat duty, reflux rate, and temperature inside the column. These parameters can be controlled using various control techniques to meet final product specification requirement as per the market demand both for large market and small market.

Various control techniques are available which can be suitably applied to get continuous controlled final product composition. Detailed process knowledge helps in control of such a nonlinear process. The control performance also affects plant processing rates and utility usage. Process control engineering helps in designing control loop system which helps in the control of multivariable system and the systems involved multiple inputs and multiple outputs.

5.1 Steps to achieve quality specifications

5.1.1 Fixing product specifications

A specification is the minimum requirement according to which a producer or service provider makes and delivers the product and service to the customer.

5.1.2 Deciding on the method of manufacture

Design and implementation of method of manufacture in actual plant condition permit to make product in the quickest and easiest way of manufacturing. These also require preparing manufacturing instructions, sequence of operations, and other procedures.

5.1.3 Providing the necessary machines, plant, tooling, and other equipment

Everything that is required for manufacture must be selected, taking care that all the elements are capable of achieving the standard of quality demanded.

6. Benefits

Benefits of reactive distillation include:

- Increased speed of operation
- Lower costs—reduced equipment use, reduced energy use, and handling being easy
- Less waste and fewer by-products
- Improved product quality—reducing opportunity for degradation because of less heat requirement

7. Modeling of heterogeneous catalyzed packed RDC

Modeling of RD column involves basic concept of distillation column carrying out reaction in a reactive zone in between the rectifying zone and stripping zone [18–21]. Thus modeling can be represented by various balances for different zones of reactive distillation column. Non-equilibrium modeling was carried out for heterogeneous catalyzed packed RDC using first principle approach. The schematic view of heterogeneous packed RDC is shown in **Figure 2**.

The basic assumptions for this model are as follows:

1. Constant relative volatility of the components
2. Constant liquid hold up in reactive zone, reboiler, and condenser
3. Assuming reactive zone to be a single stage
4. Negligible vapor holdup
5. Thorough mixing of vapor and liquid

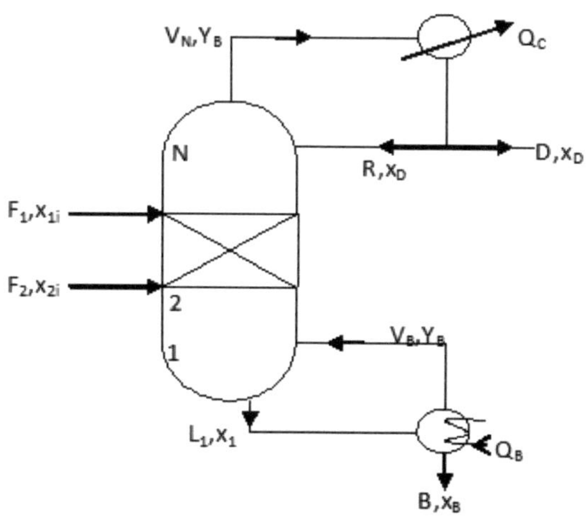

Figure 2.
Schematic diagram of packed RDC.

7.1 Component material balance

Figure 3 gives flow of vapor and liquid over a plate/tray. As per the reaction of two reactants producing two products, component material balance for various sections of the column can be written as follows:

1. Rectifying and stripping trays

$$\frac{d(x_{n,j}M_n)}{dt} = L_{n+1}x_{n+1,j} + V_{n-1}\,y_{n-1,j} - L_n x_{n,j} - V_n\,y_{n,j} \tag{1}$$

2. Reactive trays

$$\frac{d(x_{n,j}M_n)}{dt} = L_{n+1}x_{n+1,j} + V_{n-1}\,y_{n-1,j} - L_n x_{n,j} - V_n\,y_{n,j} + R_{n,j} \tag{2}$$

3. Feed trays

$$\frac{d(x_{n,j}M_n)}{dt} = L_{n+1}x_{n+1,j} + V_{n-1}\,y_{n-1,j} - L_n x_{n,j} - V_n\,y_{n,j} + R_{n,j} + F_n z_{n,j} \tag{3}$$

4. The net reaction rate for component j on tray n in the reactive zone is given by

$$R_{n,j} = v_j M_n(k_{Fn}x_{n,A}x_{n,B} - k_{Bn}x_{n,C}x_{n,D}) \tag{4}$$

5. Reflux drum

$$\frac{d(x_{D,j}M_D)}{dt} = V_{NT}y_{NT,j} - D(1+RR)x_{D,j} \tag{5}$$

6. Column base

$$\frac{d(x_{B,j}M_B)}{dt} = L_1x_{1,j} - Bx_{B,j} - V_S y_{B,j} \tag{6}$$

7. Due to exothermic reaction, the heat of reaction vaporizes some liquid in reactive section. Therefore, the vapor rate increases in the reactive trays, and the liquid rate decreases down through the reactive trays.

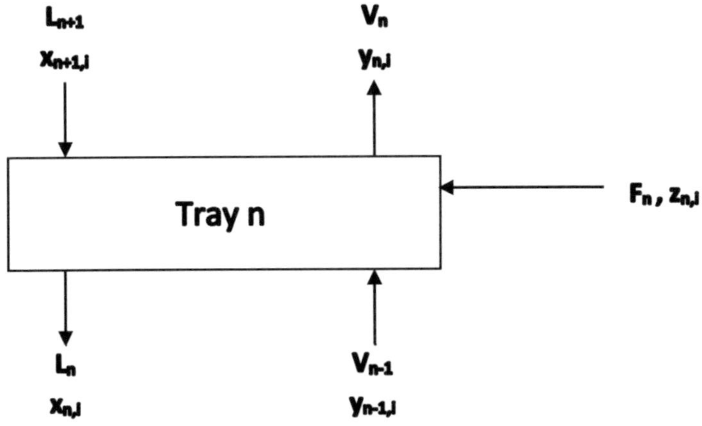

Figure 3.
Schematic of a tray/plate.

$$V_n = V_{n-1} - \frac{\lambda}{\Delta H_v} R_{n,C} \tag{7}$$

$$L_n = L_{n+1} + \frac{\lambda}{\Delta H_v} R_{n,C} \tag{8}$$

8. Vapor phase

$$\frac{dm_{iv}}{dt} = \left(V_{pi-1} * y_{pi-1}\right) - P_v - V_p + n_{ipv} \tag{9}$$

where V_{pi-1} is vapor entering the plate p, y_{pi-1} is the mole fraction of component i, and P_v is vapor added to the column, but these are leaving the column through condenser; therefore negative sign is considered, V_p is the vapor leaving the plate p, and n_{ipv} is gain of species i due to transport, i.e., mass transfer rates. It is given as.

$$\mathrm{n_{ipv}} = \int \mathrm{N_{ipv}}\, \mathrm{dp} \tag{10}$$

where N_{ip} is molar flux of species i at particular point in the two-phase dispersion.

9. Liquid phase

$$\frac{dm_{il}}{dt} = \left(L_{pi+1} * x_{pi+1}\right) - P_{Lp} - L_p - n_{ipl} - r_i * V \tag{11}$$

where L_{pi+1} is liquid entering the plate p, x_{pi+1} is the mole fraction of component i, P_{Lp} is liquid added to the column, L_p is the liquid leaving the plate p, and n_{ipl} is loss of species i due to transport, i.e., mass transfer rates. It is given as.

$$\mathrm{n_{ipl}} = \int \mathrm{N_{ipl}}\, \mathrm{dp} \tag{12}$$

where N_{ipl} is molar flux of species i at particular point in the two-phase dispersion. Since there is no accumulation at phase interphase, it follows.

$$\mathrm{M_t} = \mathrm{n_{ivp}} - \mathrm{n_{ilp}} = 0 \tag{13}$$

M_t is the accumulation due to mass transfer.

8. Case study of methyl acetate synthesis in RDC

8.1 Pilot-scale experimental results

The experimental synthesis of methyl acetate esterification was performed in pilot-scale heterogeneous catalytic packed RDC shown in **Figure 4**. The characteristics of packed RDC are given in **Table 2** and temperature data is given in **Table 3**. From the observations we conclude that the temperature of the reactive zone, from stage 3 to stage 6, lies between 50 and 70°C, which is an ideal condition for production of methyl acetate catalytic esterification reaction. The temperature of stripping zone lies between 50 and 59°C. Temperature of rectifying section lies between 30 and 45°C.

Figure 4.
Pilot-scale reactive distillation column.

Contents	Characteristics and conditions	
No. of stages	10 including reboiler and condenser	
Rectifying section	7–8	
Reactive section	3–6	
Stripping section	1–2	
Packing used	HYFLUX	
Catalyst	Amberlyst-15 (Acidic ion-exchange)	
Catalyst granularity	10–100 μm	
Average particle diameter (m)	7.4×10^{-4}	
Apparent density (g/cm^3)	0.99	
Macro porosity of catalyst	0.32	
Condenser type	Total condenser	
Feed	Methanol	Acetic acid
• Feed stage • Feed temperature • Feed pressure • Feed flow rate (L/min)	3 50°C Atmospheric 0.03	6 50°C Atmospheric 0.03
Reflux ratio	5	

Table 2.
Characteristics of packed reactive distillation column.

We have set the reboiler temperature at 70°C which is close to boiling point of methanol. However it varies as the reaction proceeds. The composition of methyl acetate obtained experimentally is 96%. The pressure of the top stage varies between 108 and 163 mmHg and that of reboiler varies between 249 and 300 mmHg.

Time (min)	Temperature profile (°C)								Pressure (mmHg)		Reboiler temp (°C)
	T1	T2	T3	T4	T5	T6	T7	T8	P1	P8	
10	53	52	42	43	41	36	33	22	108	280	66
20	52	56	49	53	51	50	42	27	138	293	66
30	55	57	52	55	55	51	41	30	115	270	70
40	56	56	54	55	61	52	42	40	115	270	70
50	57	55	52	56	61	52	44	41	117	272	69
60	56	59	55	57	68	54	43	40	138	270	72
70	57	58	55	56	65	52	44	40	114	273	70
80	58	59	56	60	64	56	45	40	115	249	66.4
90	58	59	57	60	56	57	40	41	115	249	68
100	56	59	55	57	60	51	44	40	169	300	70
110	56	55	51	55	60	48	42	40	163	295	72
120	56	55	51	55	60	49	43	40	163	294	72

Table 3.
Experimental results of methyl acetate synthesis.

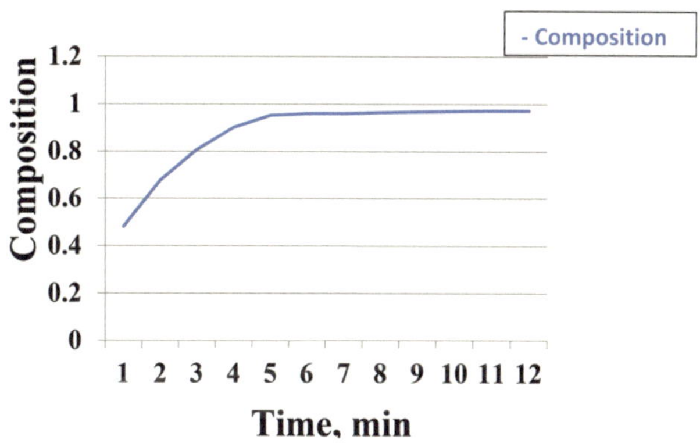

Figure 5.
Variation in product composition WRT time.

It is obvious that the product composition continuously increases with respect to time and as soon as concentration of reactants decreases, the composition also decreases. For continuous process, continuous supply of reactants is required to maintain the product composition. The variation of composition with time is shown in **Figure 5**.

9. Simulation and optimization

Simulation and optimization are the act of obtaining the best result under given circumstances. Optimization can be defined as the process of finding the conditions that give the maximum or minimum value of a function. Process optimization is the discipline of adjusting a process so as to optimize some specified set of parameters without violating some constraints. The chemical industry has undergone significant changes during the past 25 years due to the increased cost of energy, increasingly stringent environmental regulations, and global competition in product pricing and quality. One of the most important engineering tools for addressing these issues is optimization. Modifications in plant design and operating procedures have been implemented to reduce costs and meet constraints, with an emphasis on improving efficiency and increasing profitability. Optimal operating conditions can be implemented via increased automation at the process, plant, and company levels, often called computer-integrated manufacturing. Computers and associated software make the necessary computations feasible and cost-effective [22–25].

9.1 Steady-state simulation and optimization

Steady-state simulation of methyl acetate esterification was carried out using Aspen Plus simulator. Radfrac module, NRTL property method, and other operating conditions such as feed condition, feed location, operating pressure, column configuration including number of stages and reaction stage, type of condenser, type of reboiler, and feed flow rate of the components used are specified in Aspen Plus environment. The specification and other results are included in **Table 4**. The simulation flow sheet is shown in **Figure 6**. The product purity is attaining a highest value at the top stage. The composition profile of the column is shown in **Figure** 7. As shown in figure, the maximum composition of product methyl acetate obtained is 95.4%. The amount of methanol and acetic acid is much lower at the top of the column; this indicates the complete consumption of reactants and formation of product.

The temperature profile of the column is shown in **Figure 8**. As shown in figure, we can clearly observe that the temperature of the reactive section is higher than the other section; this is because of the exothermic nature of the esterification reaction. Also, temperature of reboiler is higher than the temperature at condenser. As it can be observed from the figure, the condenser temperature which is 57.4°C is lower than reboiler temperature which is 62.7°C. The temperature of the reactive zone is varied between 61.3 and 77.8°C, making it compatible to the exothermic nature of

Parameters	**Values**	
No. of stages	10, including reboiler and condenser	
Reactive stage	3–6 (reactive zone)	
Rectifying stage	2–3	
Stripping stage	7–9	
Input condition	Methanol	Acetic acid
Temperature	50°C	70°C
Flow rate	0.03 L/min	0.05 L/min
Reboiler heat duty	0.2 kW	
Reflux ratio	5	
Condenser temperature	57.40°C	
Distillate rate	10.56 mole/hr	
Reflux rate	52.81 mole/hr	
Reboiler temperature	62.66°C	
Bottom rate	86.12 mole/hr	
Boil up rate	23.62 mole/hr	
Boil up Ratio	0.274	

Table 4.
Input condition and result of RDC.

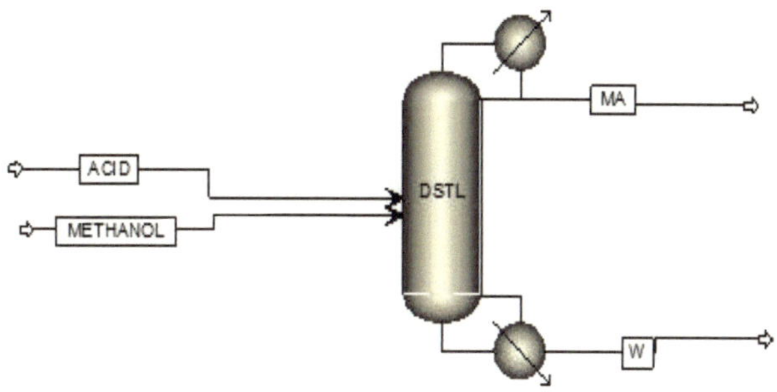

Figure 6.
Flow sheet of methyl acetate RDC.

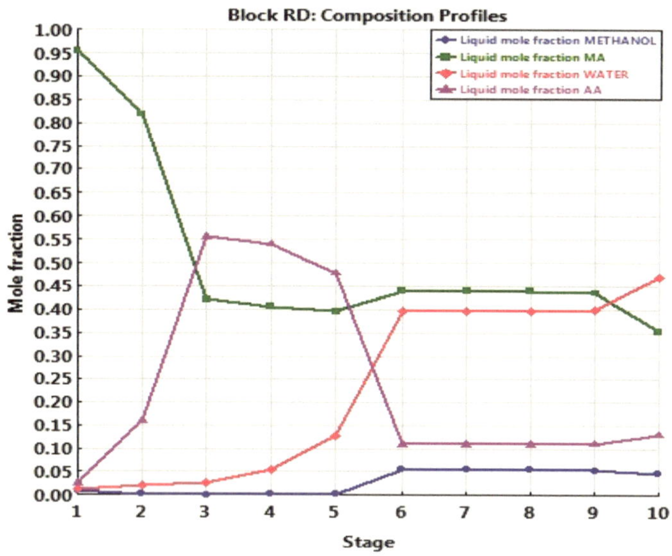

Figure 7.
Composition profile of methyl acetate RDC.

the esterification reaction. The maximum temperature of the condenser during experiment was 58°C, and the temperature of the condenser obtained from Aspen Plus was 57.4°C, which shows good agreement between experimental and simulation results.

9.2 Sensitivity analysis of methyl acetate RDC

Reactive distillation exhibits multiple steady-state conditions throughout the operation. This is known as multiplicity of the process. There are two types of multiplicity; one is known as input multiplicity, and the other is known as output multiplicity. This is the condition in which column gives same output for the different sets of process condition. In this paper, we have studied input multiplicity, in which we obtained same output for different input conditions. To analyze the situation, we have performed sensitivity analysis in Aspen Plus simulator.

For sensitivity analysis, we have first chosen molar flow of methyl acetate on the basis of heat duties whose lower and upper bounds are fixed as 1 and 3 kW, respectively. For the second case, we have calculated mass fraction of methyl acetate by

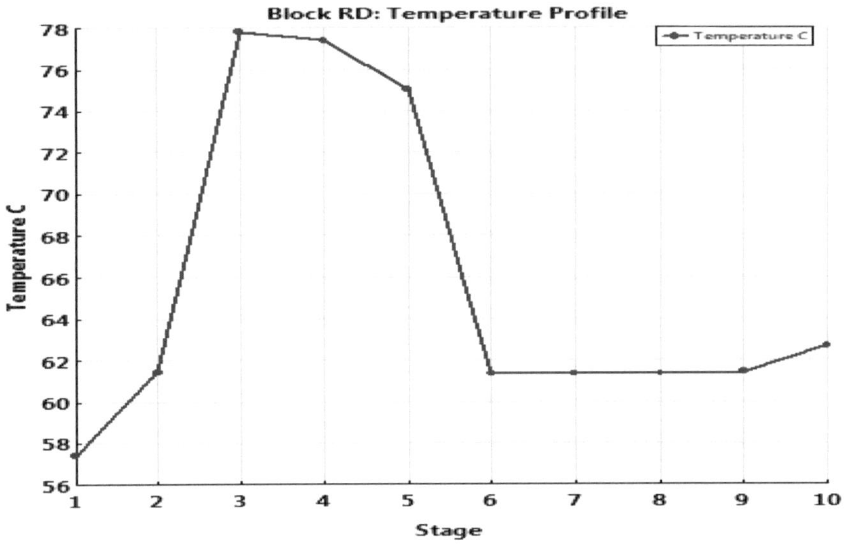

Figure 8.
Temperature profile of methyl acetate RDC.

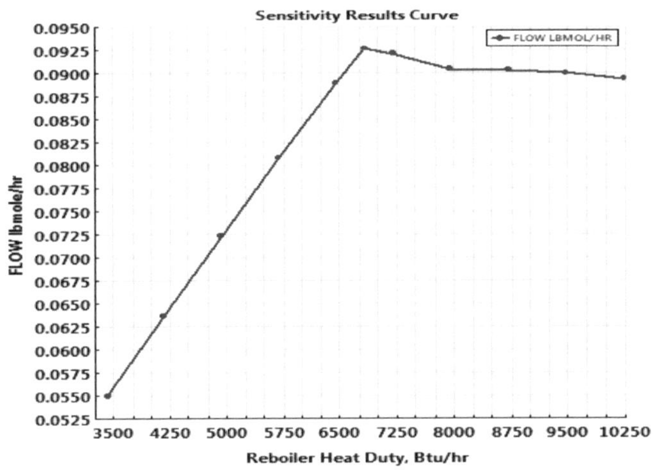

Figure 9.
Sensitivity analysis based on reboiler heat duty.

setting the molar flow of acetic acid in feed in the range of 0.01–0.08 L/min. In the third case, we have calculated distillate flow rate by varying feed flow rate in the range of 0.01–0.08 L/min to calculate the distillate-to-feed ratio (D/F). Similarly we have also calculated bottom-to-feed ratio (B/F). The result curves are shown in **Figures 9** and **10**, respectively. A shown in **Figure 9**, we can observe that the flow rate of methyl acetate is increasing as heat duty is increasing and found the maximum flow rate to be 0.927 lbmol/hr. at heat duty of 6820 Btu/hr. Similarly, we can observe that in **Figure 10**, the variation in flow rate of acetic acid is observed WRT mole fraction of product methyl acetate. The maximum product fraction is observed as 95.2% at flow rate of 0.0872 cuft/hr. The effect of change in distillate-to-feed Ratio (D/F) and change in bottom-to-feed (B/F) ratio on composition was also observed. It was found that optimized distillate-to-feed (D/F) ratio obtained 0.6275 and optimized bottom-to-feed (B/F) ratio obtained 0.4238 to get maximum product purity.

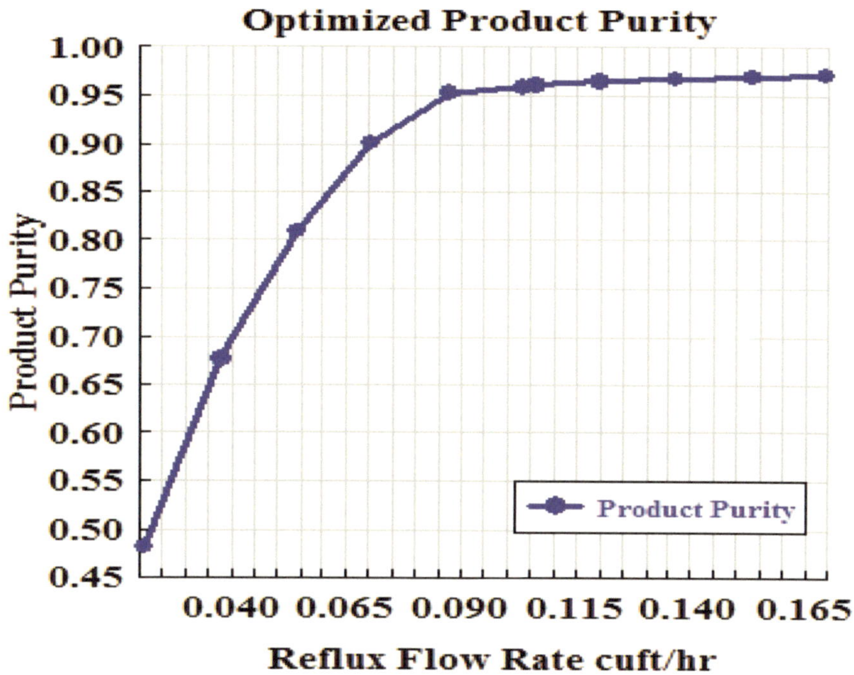

Figure 10.
Sensitivity analysis based on acid flow rate.

9.3 Optimization of methyl acetate RDC

Model analysis tool under Aspen Plus simulation facilitates optimization of the reactive distillation column. In this analysis we defined mass fraction of methyl acetate as objective on the basis of standard volumetric flow rate of acetic acid to obtain the minimum product composition that can be achieved at the top of the column. Heat duty was defined as constraint with fixed values between 1 and 3 kW

Row	Case I Variation in reboiler heat duty Btu/hr	Optimized flow rate of methyl acetate lbmol/hr	Case II Variation in volumetric flow rate of acetic acid, ft^3/hr	Optimized product composition
1	3412.14	0.0549	0.0211	0.4808
2	4170.39	0.0637	0.0376	0.6776
3	4928.64	0.0723	0.05414	0.8070
4	5686.90	0.0807	0.07062	0.9011
5	6445.15	0.0888	0.08710	0.9522
6	6824.28	0.0926	0.10358	0.9596
7	7203.41	0.0920	0.10594	0.9604
8	7961.66	0.0904	0.12006	0.9643
9	8719.91	0.0902	0.13655	0.9676
10	9478.17	0.0900	0.15303	0.9700
11	10236.42	0.0893	0.16951	0.9719

Table 5.
Summary of the sensitivity and optimization results.

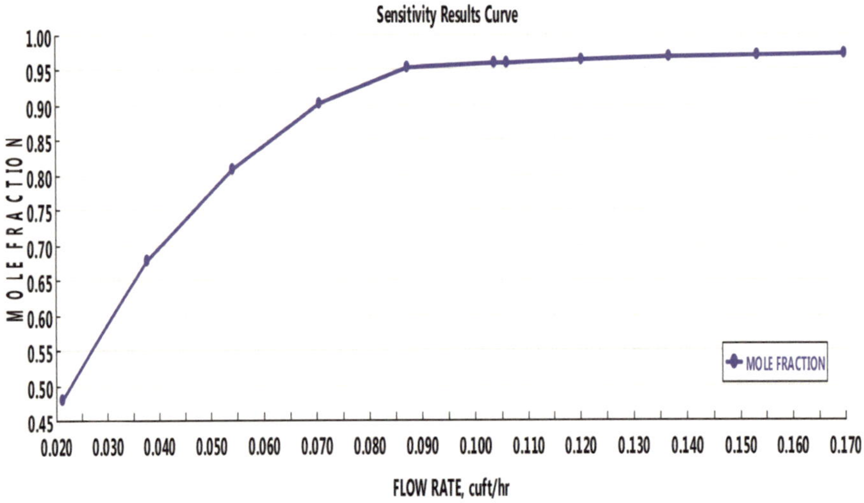

Figure 11.
Sensitivity curve for optimized flow rate and composition.

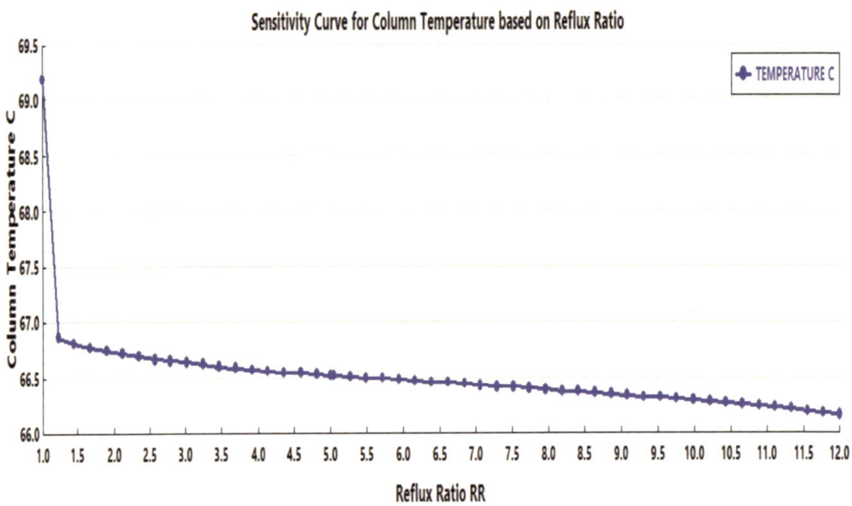

Figure 12.
Sensitivity curve for column temperature based on reflux ratio.

as lower and upper limits, respectively. After the optimization, we obtained 26.99% as the minimum composition of methyl acetate and 2 kW as the required optimized heat duty.

The summary of optimization and sensitivity results obtained from Aspen Plus simulation is included in **Table 5**. The optimized value of reboiler heat duty obtained was 2 kW, and optimized reflux ratio obtained was 4.69. These values are close to the experimental values which again show good agreement between experimental and simulation studies. The optimized flow rate of methyl acetate obtained using reboiler heat duty as manipulated variable is 0.093 lbmol/hr., and optimized product fraction obtained using standard volumetric flow rate of acetic acid is 0.96. The sensitivity result curve for optimized flow rate and composition of methyl acetate is shown in **Figure 11**, and sensitivity result curve for variation in column temperature based on reflux flow is shown in **Figure 12**.

10. Conclusion

This chapter gives details of reactive distillation as effective unit for various synthesis and manufacturing. The detailed case study envisaged to produce methyl acetate using methanol and acetic acid in a pilot plant reactive distillation column. The operating conditions were maintained as feed temperature of 50°C, column pressure of 1 atmosphere, feed rate of 0.03 L/min, and initial reboiler temperature of 70°C. The experiment yielded high purity of methyl acetate. We have succeeded in obtaining 95% purity of methyl acetate. The experimentation was then followed by simulations so as to contrast the results. The Aspen Plus simulation gives methyl acetate purity of 91.1%. This was followed by validation of results using sensitivity and optimization analysis. The optimized value of reflux was obtained as 4.69 and required reboiler duty 2 kW. The sensitivity analysis registered distillation-to-feed (D/F) ratio as 0.6275 and bottom-to-feed (B/F) ratio 0.4235 to obtain maximum product purity. These encouraging results establish a good agreement between experimental and simulation studies.

Nomenclature

v_j	stoichiometric coefficient
$R_{n,j}$	reaction rate on *n*th stage
M_n	liquid holdup on *n*th stage
k_{Fn}	forward reaction rate on *n*th stage
k_{Bn}	backward reaction rate on *n*th stage
$x_{n,j}$	liquid composition on *n*th stage
V_n	flow rate of vapor on *n*th stage
L_n	flow rate of liquid on *n*th stage
λ	heat of reaction
ΔH_v	net heat of vaporization
NT	total number of stages
D	distillate flow rate
B	bottoms flow rate
$y_{n,j}$	vapor composition on *n*th stage
RR	reflux ratio
F_n	feed flow rate on *n*th stage
$z_{n,j}$	feed composition on *n*th stage
P_j^S	pure component vapor pressure
T_n	temperature at *n*th stage
P	total pressure

Author details

Vandana Sakhre
Department of Chemical Engineering, School of Engineering and IT,
Manipal Academy of Higher Education (MAHE), Dubai, UAE

*Address all correspondence to: vandana.sakhre@manipaldubai.com

References

[1] Agreda VH, Partin LR. Reactive distillation process for the production of methyl acetate. US Patent; 1984. Publication number-US4435595A

[2] Ciric AR, Gu D. Synthesis of non-equilibrium reactive distillation processes by MINLP optimization. AIChe Journal, Process System Engineering. 1994;**40**:1479-1487

[3] Dohert MF, Buzad G. New tool for design of kinetically controlled reactive distillation columns for ternary mixtures. Computers and Chemical Engineering. 1995;**19**:395-408

[4] Miniotti M, Doherty MF. Design for simultaneous reaction and liquid liquid extraction. Industrial and Engineering Chemistry Research. 1998;**37**:4748-4755

[5] Subawalla H, Fair JR. Design guidelines for solid-catalyzed reactive distillation systems. Industrial and Engineering Chemistry Research. 1999; **38**(10):3696-3709

[6] Schenk MA, Gani R, Bogle D, Pistikopoulos EN. A hybrid modeling approach for separation systems involving distillation, Chemical Engineering Research and Design Part A. 1999;**77**:519-534

[7] Cardoso MF, Salcedo RL. Optimization of reactive distillation processes with simulated annealing. Chemical Engineering Science. 2000;**55**: 5059-5078

[8] Taylor R, Krishna R. Reactive distillation: Status and future directions. In: Modeling of Homogeneous and Heterogeneous Reactive Distillation Processes; Chapter 9; Reactive Distillation: Status and Future Directions, Wiley Online. 2002;215-240

[9] Almeida CP, Swinkels PLJ. Designing reactive distillation processes: Present and future. Computers & Chemical Engineering;**28**(10):1997-2020

[10] Harmsem GJ. Reactive distillation: The front-runner of industrial process intensification: A full review of commercial applications, research, scale-up, design and operation. Chemical Engineering and Processing. 2007;**46**:774-780

[11] Luo H-P, Xiao W-D. A reactive distillation process for a cascade and azeotropic reaction system: Carbonylation of ethanol with dimethyl carbonate. Chemical Engineering Science. 2001;**56**:403-410

[12] Güttinger TE, Morari M. Predicting multiple steady states in equilibrium reactive distillation. 1. Analysis of nonhybrid systems. Industrial and Engineering Chemistry Research. 1999; **38**:1633

[13] Güttinger TE, Morari M. Predicting multiple steady states in equilibrium reactive distillation. 2. Analysis of hybrid systems. Industrial and Engineering Chemistry Research. 1999; **38**:1649

[14] Bessling B, Lohning JM, Ohligschlager A, Schembecker G, Sundamacher K. Chemical Engineering Technology. 1998;**21**(5):393-400

[15] Hanika J, Kolena J, Smejkal Q. Butyl acetate via reactive distillation-modeling and experiment. Chemical Engineering Science. 1999;**54**(21): 5205-5209

[16] Hui T, Zhixian H, Ting Q, Xiaoda W, Yangxiang WU. Reactive distillation for production of n-butyl acetate: Experiment and simulation. Chinese Journal of Chemical Engineering. 2012; **20**(5):980-987

[17] Singh H, Mahajani SM, Gudi RD, Gangadwala J, Kienle A. Production of

butyl acetate by catalytic distillation: A theoretical and experimental studies. Industrial and Engineering Chemistry Research. 2005;**44**:3042-3052

[18] Katariya AM, Kamath RS, Moudgalaya KM, Mahajani SM. Non equilibrium stage modeling and nonlinear dynamic effects in the synthesis of TAME by reactive distillation. Computers and Chemical Engineering. 2008;**32**:2243-2255

[19] Kiss AA, Singh P, Strein CJG. A systematic approach towards applicability of reactive distillation. In: 21st European symposium on Computer Aided Process Engineering; 2011. pp. 191-195

[20] Bhatt K, Patel NM. Generalized modeling and simulation of reactive distillation: Esterification. Advances in Applied Science Research. 2012;**3**: 1346-1352

[21] Hounge EO. Reactive Distillation of Biodiesel: Modelling and Optimal Operation. 2013. A thesis submitted to Norwegian University of Science and Technology

[22] Lei Z, Yi C, Yang B. Design, optimization, and control of reactive distillation column for the synthesis of tert-amyl ethyl ether. Chemical Engineering Research and Design. 2013; **91**:819-830

[23] González-Rugerio CA, Fuhrmeister R, Sudhoff D, Pilarczyk J, Górak A. Optimal design of catalytic distillation columns: A case study on synthesis of TAEE. Chemical Engineering Research and Design. 2014;**92**:391-404

[24] Giwa A. Empirical modelling and optimization of PAME reactive distillation process using Minitab. International Journal of Scientific and Engineering Research. 2015;**6**:538-548

[25] Seferlis P, Grievink J. Optimal design and sensitivity analysis of a reactive distillation units using collocation models. Industrial & Engineering Chemistry Research. 2001; **40**:1673-1685